Comparative Discrimination Law

Comparative Discrimination Law

Volumes published in this Brill Research Perspectives title are listed at *brill.com/rpcd*

Comparative Discrimination Law

Age as a Protected Ground

By

Lucy Vickers

BRILL

LEIDEN | BOSTON

This paperback book edition is simultaneously published as issue 2.1 (2018) of *Comparative Discrimination Law*, DOI:10.1163/24522031-12340003.

Library of Congress Control Number: 2018951732

Typeface for the Latin, Greek, and Cyrillic scripts: "Brill". See and download: brill.com/brill-typeface.

ISBN 978-90-04-34553-9 (paperback)
ISBN 978-90-04-34554-6 (e-book)

This book is printed on acid-free paper and produced in a sustainable manner.

Contents

Comparative Discrimination Law: Age as a Protected Ground

Lucy Vickers
Oxford Brookes University, Oxford, UK
lrvickers@brookes.ac.uk

Abstract

This comparative review of age as a protected ground in discrimination law explores the underpinning questions and themes related to two main dimensions of age discrimination. The first dimension is structural, economic and labour market driven, whereby age is used to allocate a range of rights, obligations and benefits within society. The second is the social justice and equality dimension, in which age is understood as an aspect of individual identity that is worthy of protection against indignity or detriment. The review then considers the law on age discrimination in a number of jurisdictions, the EU law, the UK, Sweden, USA, Canada and South Africa, and assesses the extent to which the underpinning questions explain the developing case law.

Keywords

age discrimination – age equality – intergenerational justice

Introduction*

Age is a relative late comer to anti-discrimination law and in some respects it remains an outsider with no specialised international convention against age discrimination to support domestic or regional legal frameworks.[1] Although

* I am grateful to many colleagues who have discussed the themes in this review with me, in particular Simonetta Manfredi and Pnina Alon-Shenker. The usual disclaimer applies.

1 Age is not specifically included as an equality ground in the UDHR or ECHR, although it has been interpreted to be included in 'other status'. EU equality law only protected against age discrimination from 2000, and even then the age provisions of Directive 2000/78 included a

 | DOI:10.1163/9789004345546_002

now commonly included as a protected ground when legal systems provide protection against discrimination, this area of law has been a particular challenge to courts and legislatures as they seek to identify appropriate parameters for legal protection. Complexity and inconsistency arise because of two potentially conflicting functions of age within legal systems; on the one hand age is used as a structural mechanism for allocating a range of rights, obligations and benefits within society. Yet on the other hand, age is understood as an aspect of individual identity that is worthy of protection against indignity or detriment.

Age discrimination has a number of dimensions, structural, economic and social, which intersect with each other in a variety of ways, resulting in a complex set of concerns with which courts need to engage. An economic dimension to age discrimination is seen with its role in employment and social protection. Here age-based legislation is used to meet a number of economic needs, such as those stemming from the demographic change towards an ageing population. This change is coupled with labour market trends in some states away from working in older age, and this then creates an additional economic problem regarding sustainability of pension provision and a reduction in tax income from a shrinking working population. The resulting pressure to encourage increased participation in the workplace by older workers is combined with an additional and at times conflicting concern regarding high unemployment or under employment among younger people. In effect, age discrimination faces a 'double bind',[2] in which there is pressure to create employment for both older and younger workers in order to fulfil economic imperatives.

At the same time, age discrimination clearly raises questions which go far beyond the economic. Age equality has a clear social dimension, in which age is viewed as a characteristic, like sex, race and disability, where the law aims to end less favourable treatment, redress disadvantage and remove associated stigma. Yet, as with the economic dimension, the social dimension contains contradictions, and can so be said to encompass a second 'double bind': on the one hand, in some fundamental respects, age differs from other protected characteristics because it changes: we all start young, and hope to live to

---

longer transposition date than the protection provided in other grounds. The 1960 Canadian Bill of Rights did not include age as a protected characteristic although age is included in 1982 Charter of Fundamental Freedoms. Age is not included in the 1963 Title VII civil rights protection in the US, although age discrimination against those over 40 was protected from 1967 in separate legislation. See further, C. O'Cinnede, 'Constitutional and Fundamental Rights Aspects of Age Discrimination' in A Numhauser-Henning and M Rönnmar (eds), *Age Discrimination and Labour Law: Comparative and Conceptual Perspectives in the EU and Beyond* (Kluwer, The Netherlands, 2015).

2 F. Hendrickx 'Age and European Employment Discrimination Law' in F. Hendrickx, *Active Ageing and Labour Law* (Cambridge: Intersentia, 2012).

become old. On the other hand, age shares some fundamental similarities with other characteristics, warranting its inclusion in the protected list. As with other grounds, less favourable treatment of a group or individual on grounds of age can be viewed as an affront to individual dignity, particularly if the treatment is based on stereotypical assumptions about capacity reducing with age.

In addition, many work and social systems are infused with age related rules, such as redundancy schemes which take account of length of service, minimum ages before certain types of work are allowed, etc. Yet, it can be observed that these age limits are fairly arbitrary. Not much changes overnight between the ages of 17 to 18 which suggest that the individual's abilities change sufficiently to warrant the change in legal capacities that are then bestowed; similarly, capacity to work does not change overnight from the age of 64 to 65 when traditionally retirement has occurred.

Although age is not immutable, and changes over time, nonetheless, it can lead to disadvantageous treatment. As a result, equality law has created protections against both the economic and social disadvantages that can arise if older workers are prevented from working, or where younger workers are paid lower wages or not given work due to stereotypical assumptions about their ability to do the job. Concepts of equality based on upholding individual dignity, redressing disadvantage and overcoming stigma would seem to be apt in such situations.

These two dimensions of age discrimination, the economic aspects and the equality aspects, both contain some internal contradictions. Moreover, they intersect in various ways when age discrimination is addressed by the law; and those intersections may differ depending on the age group concerned. As a result the law is faced with many questions and conundrums: is age something that should be protected because it can be a relevant signifier of disadvantage for both the young and old? Does it matter that such disadvantages are not experienced by all members of the group? To what extent does the fact that age changes for each individual affect the way in which the law should protect this characteristic?

This assessment of the comparative approaches to age equality is divided into three main parts. In Part 1 the underpinning questions and themes related to the two main dimensions of age discrimination (the structural/economic and the social/equality) are explored. Part 2 then considers the law on age discrimination in a number of jurisdictions. Part 3 concludes with an assessment of the extent to which these underpinning questions can explain the developing case law.

Part 1: Thematic Issues

Age discrimination engages a wide and complex spectrum of issues ranging from the economic importance of all workers, old and young, having access to the workplace and other social goods, to underpinning notions of equality and social justice that require the eradication of stereotyped or assumptions or irrelevant and prejudicial categorisations. In the following sections, different aspects of the two dimensions of age equality are explored, with a view to better understanding how they should inform the development of appropriate parameters for the law on age equality.

Economic and Structural Dimensions

The first dimension of age equality to be explored is its economic dimension and its interaction with the structures of the labour market. Age is a key differential for a number of different aspects of social and working life: obvious examples include capacity to vote, marry, drive and access work. Social security benefits are also differentiated by age, with pensions paid to those over a certain age, and minimum wages and other benefits linked to the age of the claimant. In addition, labour market practices, such as the use of length of service as a criterion in redundancy decisions, lead to differential treatment related, albeit indirectly, to age. Alongside the embeddedness of age into the structures of the labour market and other social processes, the age demographic of the population has a key role in a state's economy generally as well as having a significant impact on the labour market in particular. These different elements of the economic dimension of age equality are assessed below.

Demographic Trends

Many areas of the world, including the USA and Europe, are experiencing the long term trend of an ageing population.[3] For example in the USA, by 2030, over 20 percent of the population are expected be aged 65 and over, up from 13 percent in 2010 and 9.8 percent in 1970. In Europe, increases vary according to each state, but overall the EU has seen an increase of 2.4 percent in the proportion of the population over 65 over the last decade. A similar pattern can be seen in many other countries such as Japan and Australia, although the opposite trend can be seen in many countries in Africa.[4] Where there is an increase in older persons within a population this is coupled with a reduction

3 See Jennifer M. Ortman, Victoria A. Velkoff, and Howard Hogan, An Aging Nation: The Older Population in the United States Population Estimates and Projections Current Population Reports, Issued May 2014 P25–1140, available at https://www.census.gov/prod/2014pubs/p25-1140.pdf accessed 27/10/17; and Eurostat data available at http://ec.europa.eu/eurostat/statistics-explained/index.php/Population_structure_and_ageing#Main_statistical_findings accessed 27/10/17.

4 See data produced by the World Bank at https://data.worldbank.org/indicator/SP.POP.65UP.TO.ZS accessed 27/10/17.

in the proportion of working-age persons in the population. This leads to an economic unbalance as fewer working age people are available to support the older persons in the population.

In response to the ageing of the population, many of the accepted work patterns developed over the last century in the west have been unsettled, such as an expectation that older workers will retire with pension provision to fund themselves for a relatively short number of years. Traditional pension models may be inadequate when people live longer, as pensions will need to go further. Although the assumption that an aging population has led to a pension crisis can be questioned,[5] nonetheless, it is unsurprising that one response to the increase in longevity has been the development of national and transnational policies and agendas to encourage longer working lives. For example, in the EU the year 2012 was designated the European Year for Active Ageing, and aimed to increase participation of older workers in the labour market, and encourage 'extended working lives' through the encouragement of an 'active ageing agenda'. The main legal response to this demographic trend has been the prohibition of age discrimination, discussed more below.

One might expect that the ageing of the general population would lead to a corresponding increase in participation of older workers in the work place, and in some states this trend can be seen. For example in Canada the employment rate for men aged 65 to 69 almost doubled between 2000 and 2010, and over the same period the rate for women increased from 6.9% to 16.6%.[6] However, that trend has not been replicated in other countries, and some states in Europe have seen a reduction in the length of working life, and a decline in participation in work from older workers. This reduction in participation in the workforce has significant economic effects on the sustainability of pension benefits as there are even fewer working people to support a further enlarged population of economically inactive people.[7]

At the same time as these changes in demographics and labour market participation for older people, significant changes have also occurred in the labour market participation for younger workers. High levels of unemployment as well as working poverty can be seen in the younger populations around the

5 J. Grady, Trade Unions and the Pension Crisis: Defending Member Interests in a Neoliberal World, Employee Relations, (2013) Vol. 35 No. 3: 294–308.

6 See Statistics Canada, available at https://www.statcan.gc.ca/pub/75-001-x/2011004/article/11578-eng.htm accessed 17/11/17.

7 S. Manfredi and L. Vickers, 'The Challenges of Active Ageing in the UK: A Case Study of the Approach to Retirement in the UK' in S. Manfredi and L. Vickers (ed.), *Challenges of Active Ageing: Equality Law and the Workplace*, Palgrave Macmillan UK (2016).

world. ILO statistics show that globally the youth unemployment rate rising, with the rate rising fastest in emerging countries. In developing countries the rate is more stable, but the absolute numbers of unemployed youth is expected to rise due to an expanding labour force. In developed countries, the rate of unemployment is highest. Moreover, even for those in work, job quality is a concern: many young people are working, but at wages which will not lift them out of poverty. Indeed, younger people experience a higher incidence of working poverty or relative poverty than other adults. In addition young people frequently work in informal, part-time or temporary jobs and are doing so involuntarily.[8]

The statistics on youth employment show that while the population is ageing, younger people are experiencing particular difficulties in accessing the labour market, either at all, or on equal terms with older workers. The high levels of under- or unemployment among young people can lead to conflict between generations, whereby older workers are understood to block the employment prospects of younger workers by remaining in their jobs into older age. What is termed 'intergenerational justice' then requires that older workers should hand their jobs on to younger workers in order to give them a fair chance in life. This approach has been criticised as based on a flawed economic model and remains contested,[9] but, nonetheless, the potential for conflict between different age groups remains a concern for those developing polices to manage age discrimination.

A further aspect of the demographics associated with age relates to the interaction of age, both youth, and older age, with poverty.[10] The high rates of under- and unemployment for youth will lead to a strong correlation between youth and poverty, as under- or unemployment reduces young people's ability to support themselves economically. Clearly this will have a long term impact as their economic outlook will be diminished by their impoverished start to working life. Moreover, the effects are likely to endure as they will be unlikely to be able to start a process of saving for older age. In older age the pattern is repeated, whereby shorter working lives and increased longevity can lead to

---

8 See the ILO World Employment Social Outlook: Trends for Youth 2106 report http://www.ilo.org/wcmsp5/groups/public/---dgreports/---dcomm/---publ/documents/publication/wcms_513739.pdf accessed 30/10/17.

9 S. Fredman, 'The Age of Equality; in S. Fredman and S. Spencer, *Age as an Equality Issue: Legal and Policy Perspectives* (Oxford: Hart Publishing, 2003) at p. 46.

10 See Income Poverty in Old Age: An Emerging Development Priority, UN Department of Economic and Social Affairs, Programme on Ageing, available at: http://www.un.org/esa/socdev/ageing/documents/PovertyIssuePaperAgeing.pdf accessed 30/10/17.

poverty in old age. However, the correlation of poverty with older age is not straightforward. For example, in the UK, while levels of poverty among the over 70s is high, equally a subset of the over 65s have never been so wealthy.[11]

This split in the economic fortunes of the older population adds a complex layer to discussions of the economic dimension to age equality. A focus on the strong economic position of many older people can lead to a narrative in which older people are blamed for taking up more than their fair share of national resources. For example, in 2010 the UK conservative politician David Willetts (then Minister for Higher Education) argued that the baby boomer generation had taken resources away from younger generations and ought to give them back.[12] Such a narrative can create additional intergenerational conflict[13] and undermine social cohesion, as it removes sympathy for older people who live in poverty based on stereotypical assumptions that older people have never had it so good.

In sum, the data on the demographics of age is complex, multi-layered, and problematic: we have an ageing population but one that has, in some states, a shrinking engagement with the workplace; older age can correlate both with poverty and with greater wealth than in other age groups; younger workers face an employment deficit while also being needed to underpin pension provision for a greater proportion of older workers in the population. The paradoxical relationship between age and poverty means that a transparent and consistent social policy agenda on age discrimination is likely to remain elusive. Moreover, it is not even clear whether the overarching aim of the law on age discrimination should be to address the problems that relate to the interaction of age with social structures including the operation of the labour market. Instead, strong alternative reasons exist for protecting against age discrimination, reasons that relate to equality and individual dignity, rather than to issues of poverty and labour market access. These are discussed as part of the second dimension of age discrimination below. First, two further structural aspects of age discrimination are considered.

---

11 C. D'Arcy & L. Gardiner, The Generation of Wealth: Asset accumulation across and within cohorts (June 2017) available at http://www.resolutionfoundation.org/app/uploads/2017/06/Wealth.pdf accessed 30/10/17.

12 D. Willetts, *The Pinch: How the Baby Boomers Took their Children's Future—And How they can Give it Back* (Atlantic Books, 2010).

13 A. Numhauser-Henning, An Introduction to Elder Law and the Norma Elder Law Research Environment, Different Approaches to Elder Law (2013) The Norma Research Programme Faculty of Law Lund University.

Age Equality and the Labour Market

In many respects, age is institutionalised in the structures of the labour market. Age infuses many aspects of the labour market, and age related rules and practices can be seen in many areas, most fundamentally in relation to restrictions on child labour and the acceptance of retirement rules. Numerous other examples can be found, some of which have since been challenged in the courts: Italy imposed limits on the use of zero hours contracts, but not for those under 25 and over 55, in order to encourage their employment;[14] in Germany fixed term contracts were limited for those under 52, but no objective reason was needed for those over 52;[15] and in the UK redundancy payment rates vary by age with those over 40 receiving higher rates of redundancy compensation. Moreover, many employers allow for incremental pay scales which increase with length of service, which is, of course, linked indirectly with age.[16]

Many of these policies and practices can be justified if age discrimination is understood from an economic perspective. Some practices reflect the idea that different age groups have different needs at different career stages. Thus, flexibility or lower wages at the start of a career may make a worker more attractive to employers, given their relative lack of experience which could otherwise act as a hindrance to gaining employment. Alternatively, age related rules may be the result of collective bargaining and reflect the wishes of those in work (e.g. increased pay with long service), and redundancy selection processes that reward long service (e.g. 'last in first out'). Other rules, such as enhanced redundancy payments for older workers, reflect a concern to protect older workers from the hardships of an ageist employment market and a concern that older workers may find it difficult to find new work.

Whilst it is arguable that these practices reflect ageist assumptions and should be rooted out if age equality is to be achieved, age infused labour market structures may in fact reflect the wishes of most workers, and create a fair structure when viewed across the whole of a career, or across the complete course of a person's life.[17]

---

14 See *Abercrombie & Fitch Italia Srl v. Antonino Bordonaro* Case C143/16, decision of AG Bobek on 23 March 2017.

15 *Mangold* (C-144/04) decision of the CJEU of 22 November 2005.

16 *Cadman v Health and Safety Executive* Case C-17/05.

17 See D. McKerlie, 'Equality and Time' (1989) 99 *Ethics* 475, and G. Cupit, 'Justice, Age, and Veneration' (1998) 108 *Ethics* 702 cited in R Horton, 'Justifying Age Discrimination in the EU' in U. Belavusau and K. Henrard, *EU Anti-Discrimination Law beyond Gender* (Hart Publishing, Oxford, 2018).

One justification for increasing wages over time is explored by Jolls,[18] who suggests that the increase in wages over time only partially reflects increased productivity. Higher wages are also justified as a way to incentivise workers and to reflect individuals' psychological preference for improved wages over time. In effect, pay is back loaded, with lower wages paid compared to productivity in the early years of a career, compensated by the payment of higher wages compared to productivity in later years.[19] This uneven wage/work bargain has generally been accepted by workers, who prefer to see their wages increase steadily over time, and is reflected in many collectively bargained salary schemes. This bargain only works if employers keep to their side of the bargain and continue to pay the higher wage premium in the second half of people's careers. Thus, according to Jolls, the justification of age discrimination legislation is that it ties employers' hands, ensuring that they continue to employ workers once they are enjoying the high wage phase of employment. This way of understanding the structure of wages and employment can be used to justify some elements of age discrimination in wages on the basis that it benefits the generality of workers over all, and is fair if understood across the whole life course.

However work structures based on age differentials for wages are not problem-free, and may not be fair when viewed from an individual perspective. They are based on one particular model of employment in which workers have job security across fairly long working lives. Those who have taken career breaks, or who have entered the workforce later, may not benefit from the higher wages for long enough to compensate for lower wages earlier on. Moreover, the model assumes that the period during which the highest rates are paid will end with retirement at a set age. Without retirement, older workers can work indefinitely at the higher premium level for longer than originally set at the start of the bargain, and they will end up over paid across their careers.

Thus if incremental rises in wages over time are to work fairly, they must be coupled with the use of retirement at a pre-agreed time, so that the periods of under- and over-payment compared to productivity are balanced out. Yet, as discussed below, compulsory retirement remains contentious as it involves unequal treatment on grounds of age.

Moreover, this model only works as long as it is adopted across the whole of the labour market: older workers will only deserve the higher premium pay if

18 C. Jolls, 'Hands-tying and the Age Discrimination in Employment Act' (1996) 74 Tex. L. Rev. 1813.

19 E.P. Lazear, "Why Is There Mandatory Retirement?" (1979) 87 *Journal of Political Economy* 1261–84.

is balanced against lower pay earlier on in their careers; if workers do not work for long enough at the higher rate, they will have been under paid across their careers; and employers will only be able to afford to pay the higher wages of older workers if all employers are bound into the same structures. But if the labour market structure on which this is based is disrupted, then the process will break down. The introduction of new flexible, or precarious, approaches to employment, discussed below, sees just this disruption of the traditional labour market, and this has consequences for wages and employment security. The impact can be seen on all workers, with particular effects on younger and older workers.

Changes in the Organisation of Work

Age based structures in the labour market can more easily be justified when standard forms of employment trajectory are assumed, in which staff enjoy long uninterrupted careers, ending in retirement at a prearranged age. Recent changes to the standard form contract have challenged this model. In particular, increased flexibility in labour market structures and changes in the way in which the law treats retirement have a number of consequences which relate to age discrimination. The interaction of pay schemes that are structured around age, with new forms of employment and changes in the law relating to retirement, discussed next, create a complex dimension to debates on the correct parameters of age discrimination.

Move to Precarious and Flexible Work

Changes in the organisation of work have been widespread over recent years, with an increase in flexible and non-standard modes of working,[20] in particular the growth of zero-hours contracts and the rise of the 'gig'[21] and 'collaborative' economy.[22] The change away from traditional labour market structures to more flexible, but at the same precarious, working structures can be explained as a response to deregulatory politics and economics, which have resulted in deregulation in a number of areas including the labour market. This deregulatory turn in the labour market, leaves many workers vulnerable: the impact on

---

20 For a review of changes to employment law in Europe see N Countouris, M Freedland (eds), *Resocialising Europe in a Time of Crisis* (Cambridge, CUP, 2013).

21 J. Prassl, M. Risak, 'Uber, Taskrabbit, and Co.: Platforms as Employers-Rethinking the Legal Analysis of Crowdwork' (2015) 37 Comp. Lab. L. & Pol'y J. 619.

22 See C. Codagnone and B. Martens, *Scoping the Sharing Economy: Origins, Definitions, Impact and Regulatory Issues* (European Commission, 2016) available at https://ec.europa.eu/jrc/sites/jrcsh/files/JRC100369.pdf (accessed 8 December 2017).

women has been noted by Fredman,[23] and to this can be added workers whose vulnerability is based on age, both younger and older workers.

As seen above, the number of young people who are under-employed is growing, and one of the causes is an increase in precarious jobs, in which job security as it is traditionally understood is markedly reduced. For example, the gig economy, where work is made available through 'platform sharing,' operates outside of traditional employment contract:[24] payment is made per job completed, and there is no notion of incremental pay that rewards long service, working time protections, or health and safety rules, let alone redundancy or unfair dismissal rules. Zero-hours contracts and other forms of precarious work also leave staff vulnerable to downturns in work, effectively moving most of the risks in the enterprise from the employer to the service provider, who is at times denied even the more limited protection available to workers.

Although these trends affect the workforce as a whole, the rise in precarious work can be seen to have a particular impact on workers who face any additional vulnerability in the workplace, including those at risk of discrimination on any grounds including age. Indeed, flexible working arrangements such as fixed term employment, and internships (often unpaid) are commonly offered to young people as a way to promote their entry into the workplace, at a stage when they may lack the competitive edge given their lack of experience in comparison with older workers.[25] Under the traditional labour market conditions, such workers would have expected to transition to more stable employment later in their careers, but the increase in the non-traditional types of work can mean that workers either get stuck in precarious work, or lose their employment to be replaced by younger workers. This pattern is likely to create problems in later life, if insufficient stable employment results in reduced or non-existent pension provision.

The increase in precarious work also has an impact on older workers. First, for those who have participated in traditional labour market structures, a shift to payment per job results in an injustice if they have been paid below market rates for some part of their careers on the expectation of increased pay later

23 S. Fredman, 'Women at Work: The Broken Promise of Flexicurity' (2004) 33 (4) *Industrial Law Journal* 299–319.

24 Although recent case law in the UK suggests that those working for the gig economy should be classified as workers. *Uber v Aslam and others* [2017] UKEAT 0056_17_1011.

25 See M. Rönnmar, 'Age Discrimination and Labour Law, a comparative analysis' in A. Numhauser-Henning and M. Rönnmar (eds), *Age Discrimination and Labour Law: Comparative and Conceptual Perspectives in the EU and Beyond* (Kluwer, The Netherlands, 2015).

on. Second, for those for whom ageing means a reduced capacity to work, any change in employment is likely to involve a move to more precarious types of employment. The removal of retirement as a mechanism available to employers to manage performance (discussed below) may mean that older workers looking for work are likely to be offered fixed term work rather than permanent work.

Shifts in the organisation of work can give rise to a second type of difficulty when addressing age discrimination. Where employers seek to dismantle parts of their organisational structures that are potentially age-discriminatory, such as age related pay structures, comparative unfairness will develop between the terms and conditions of workers of different ages. For example where a workplace pays using a deferred benefits system whereby pay increases over time without a tight correlation to performance, the system only remains fair if it continues for the full working lifetime of the individual, so that they get the correct amount of compensatory higher pay. If these structures are changed, injustice can arise: either over payment if compulsory retirement is removed; or under payment if payment of strict market value payments are made, as is likely to happen if workers are paid by the job as happens particularly under the gig economy.

The complexity of introducing changes to the organisational structures of work has a significant impact on the operation of the law on age discrimination. Straightforward concepts of formal equality, understood as same treatment for workers of different ages are likely to be inadequate to the task of achieving fairness. Instead, courts will need to be sensitive to the fact that changes in working structures can benefit and disadvantage different groups of workers at different stages of their working lives.

Retirement and Age Discrimination

As well as changes towards greater flexibility in the organisation of work, changes have also taken place with regard to retirement. The assumption that workers will retire has played an important role in many organisations,[26] and continues to affect organisations and individuals in terms of performance management systems, workforce planning, individual career choices and personal and institutional financial planning. The prohibition on age discrimination, taken with the demographic changes outlined above, has created particular challenges for the management of the traditional approach to retirement.

26 See C. Kilpatrick, 'The New UK Retirement Regime, Employment Law and Pensions' (2008) 37 ILJ 1 for discussion of the history and development of retirement and pensions.

In terms of workforce demographics, as noted above, trends have varied with some states seeing an increase in numbers working beyond traditional retirement ages, and others seeing trends towards early retirement. In addition, states regulate retirement in very different ways: some states allow mandatory retirement, others such as the UK and Canada, have abolished the practice. Other states impose mandatory retirement on the public sector, or allow collective agreements to impose retirement ages across whole sectors of employment.[27]

The ways in which different states have responded to the issue of retirement is discussed further in later sections, together with the ways in which social and economic dimensions interact in the case of retirement. At this stage, it is worth noting that changes in retirement practice form a key aspect of the structural changes currently taking place in the organisation of the labour market.

Conclusions on the Structural Dimension of the Labour Market

The economic and structural dimension to age equality reveals a complex set of factors likely to influence its legal treatment. The legal framework governing age discrimination operates in a context of significant change, not only in terms of the demographics of the workplace, but also in terms of the organisation of work from standard work contracts to more flexible forms of work. These changes create a significant challenge to those interpreting the legal framework. Yet the complexity facing courts is compounded by debates concerning the social dimension of age equality, in which fundamental questions are raised regarding why and on what basis age is included in the list of protected characteristics in equality law. It is this second dimension of age equality that is discussed next.

The Social Dimension of Age Equality

Although age discrimination raises a range of economic issues, it nonetheless retains, at its core, notions of social justice. Older people can be subjected to stigma, detrimental treatment, ageist stereotypes and social exclusion; young people are also subjected to stereotypes and often less favourable treatment in terms and conditions of employment. To the extent that these disadvantages are linked to age, it can be seen that, although a late comer to equality law, age discrimination sits clearly within an equality framework and should share its general aims.

---

27 See 'A comparative analysis of non-discrimination law in Europe 2016' (European Equality Law Network, Luxembourg: Publications Office of the European Union, 2016).

However, even here there is room for debate, as the meaning of the term 'equality', and hence the aims of equality law have been the subject of extensive academic debate.[28] It is not intended to consider the debate in detail here, but rather to consider the implications of that debate for age discrimination.

At its most basic, equality can be understood in formal or symmetrical terms, requiring that like cases be treated alike, but such an approach has limitations, in particular the difficulty in determining when two cases are alike. The problem of finding appropriate comparators has long created difficulties for equality law, leading Westen[29] famously to argue that equality is an empty or at least a circular concept. This can be coupled with concerns that like treatment can be achieved by a levelling down of benefits when equality is claimed, thus denying everyone a benefit rather than extending it to all.[30]

The shortcomings of the formal equality concept have led to the development of more substantive concepts of equality. The model discussed here is based on Fredman's proposed four-fold approach to equality, which draws on insights from current debates on the meaning of equality. Her model envisages that equality should aim to: redress disadvantage; recognise the importance of individual dignity and identity and tackle stereotype and stigma; address social exclusion and promote participation; and achieve structural change to accommodate difference.[31] Such an approach involves a social model of equality in which the focus is not only on the physical capacities associated with particular characteristics, but with the way in which society treats the individual.

Applying the substantive concept of equality to age discrimination suggests that, to the extent that age is related to disadvantage, stigma, the infringement of dignity and social exclusion, it should be included within the protection of equality law. Where such aims are met, protection against age discrimination can be justified despite the fact that age is in some respects different from other protected characteristics (most obviously because everyone has an age,

---

28 See for example, C. O'Cinneide, 'Fumbling Towards Coherence: The Slow Evolution of Equality and Anti-Discrimination Law in Britain' (2006) NILQ 57, C. Barnard and B. Hepple, 'Substantive Equality' (2000) 59 CLJ 562, S. Fredman, *Discrimination Law* (Oxford: OUP, 2002), B. Hepple, 'The Aims of Equality Law' in C. O'Cinneide and J. Holder (eds) *Current Legal Problems* (Oxford: OUP, 2008).

29 See P. Westen, 'The Empty Idea of Equality' (1982) 95 Harv. L.R. 537.

30 See for example, C. Barnard and B. Hepple, 'Substantive Equality' (2000) 59 *CLJ* 562 and S. Fredman, Discrimination Law (Oxford, OUP, 2002).

31 H. Collins, 'Discrimination, Equality and Social Inclusion' (2003) 66 *MLR* 16, S. Fredman, The Future of Equality In Britain, EOC, Working Paper Series No. 5, (London, Equal Opportunities Commission 2002) 11, S. Fredman, 'Substantive Equality Revisited' (2016) 14(3) International Journal of Constitutional Law 712.

and it changes over time). However, the reverse is also true: where these aims are not met, perhaps because the treatment serves a purely economic aim, unequal treatment on the basis of age may be justified.

Aspects of the aims of equality law are considered in what follows, in order to assess the strength of the social dimensions of equality as it applies to age. As with the economic dimension to age equality, the social dimension will also be seen to contain contradictions and complexities, meaning that the social egalitarian case against age discrimination is not clear cut.

Dignity

Moving beyond the concept of equality as being about achieving same treatment, a clear alternative aim for equality law is to uphold individual dignity and identity. The concept of dignity is well established as foundational in human rights law[32] and is based on the idea that humans all have an essential dignity and should be treated, in Kant's terms, as ends rather than means.[33] Dignity is underpinned by the moral judgment that humans are of intrinsic, incomparable and indelible worth, independent of their abilities or accomplishments.[34] The idea that human beings can expect others to respect the dignity inherent in their humanity is one that has been agreed virtually universally, perhaps most famously in the Universal Declaration of Human Rights: 'All human beings are born free and equal in dignity and rights'.[35]

One benefit of basing the idea of equality on the foundation of dignity is that it creates room to provide broader recognition[36] for different identifies. It encompasses the idea that equality and dignity can mean more than just the equalising of benefits and advantages as between different people, but can involve recognition of the uniqueness of individuals, and their distinctiveness. The concept of 'recognition' in this sense is based on the view that in order to realise human dignity, autonomy and equality fully, humans need to be able to develop a sense of personal identity and to have that identity recognised,

32 For further discussion see C. McCrudden (ed.), *Understanding Human Dignity* (Oxford, OUP, 2013).

33 E. Kant, *The Moral Law: Kant's Groundwork of the Metaphysics of Morals* (HJ Paton, trans) (London, Hutchinson, 1963).

34 D. Réaume, 'Discrimination and Dignity' (2003) 63 *Louisiana LR* 645, 675.

35 Art 1. Dignity also features in the preamble to the United Nations Charter, and the preambles of the ICCPR and the ICESCR.

36 See N. Fraser, 'Rethinking Recognition' (2000) *3* New Left Review 107 and C. Taylor, *Multiculturalism and The Politics of Recognition* (1992, Princeton University Press, Princeton).

respected and valued. Thus equality demands that that the self-respect and sense of self-worth of individuals is preserved.[37]

Whilst aiming to uphold individual dignity may be a laudable aim, it is worth noting that the concept has been challenged as a foundational basis for equality and human rights in general. Moreover, in particular respects it may provide an inadequate theoretical underpinning for laws prohibiting age discrimination.

In general terms, dignity can be understood to be just as empty a concept as equality, ready to be filled by a wide range of meanings not all of which will be honourable.[38] Indeed, as Fredman points out, dignity is capable of being understood in a hierarchical way, and has its history in ideas of rank and hierarchy.[39] Furthermore, Gearty suggests that the range of meanings makes the concept of dignity susceptible to being used by those already in power, to assert their interests against the democratic will.[40] This would seem to have particular resonance in the case of age, as the main beneficiaries of age discrimination protection in the US have been older white men in relatively high status and highly paid jobs.[41]

A further critique of dignity arguments is that dignity can be understood in individualised terms and can thus be used to undermine more community based goods. Again the argument has resonance in respect to age, where the use of retirement may work as a communal good if it increases the access of younger workers to the labour market, but it may at the same time infringe individual dignity.[42]

---

37 Rawls identifies self-respect as a 'primary good'. A Theory Of Justice (Oxford, OUP, 1999, revised edition).

38 C. Douzinas, *Human Rights and Empire: The Political Philosophy of Cosmopolitanism* (Abingdon, Routledge-Cavnendish, 2007) cited in C. McCrudden (ed.) *Understanding Human Dignity* (Oxford, OUP, 2013); and R. O'Connell, The role of dignity in equality law; lessons from Canada and South Africa (2008) 6(2) International J. Constitutional law 267.

39 S. Fredman, 'Substantive Equality Revisited' (2016) 14(3) International Journal of Constitutional Law 712.

40 C. Gearty, 'Socio-Economic Rights, Basic Needs, and Human Dignity: A Perspective from Law's Front Line' in C. McCrudden (ed.) *Understanding Human Dignity* (Oxford, OUP, 2013).

41 G. Rutherglen, 'From Race to Age: the Expanding Scope of Employment Discrimination Law (1995) 24(2) *The Journal of Legal Studies* 491; J.Z. Rothenberg, D.S. Gardner 'Protecting Older Workers: The Failure of the Age Discrimination in Employment Act of 1967' (2011) 38(1) *Journal of Sociology and Social Welfare* 9.

42 R. O'Connell, The role of dignity in equality law; lessons from Canada and South Africa (2008) 6(2) International J. Constitutional law 267.

The example of retirement illustrates the difficulties in using dignity as a core aim of equality law. Compulsory retirement can be understood to undermine dignity, because work acts as a source of identity and status.[43] Denying workers access to this benefit on the basis of age, by requiring that they retire, diminishes dignity and thus infringes equality interests. However, giving dignity too much emphasis in this context may run counter to other concepts of equality. In the first place, the sense of dignity in work may not be universally experienced, but rather focused more on high status workers. Moreover, whilst an interest in the identity and status enhancing aspects of a job may be important to the individual, this may not be a sufficiently strong interest to outweigh other interests such as those of younger workers to work.[44] The competing interests of older workers to stay in work in order to maintain a sense of dignity, with the interests of younger workers to have access to the same dignity enhancing work demonstrates the limitations of using dignity as a basis for determining age discrimination cases.

Whilst the case for including age as a protected characteristic can be made on the basis of upholding dignity, the claim is not absolute. In effect, if the overriding aim of equality law is to uphold dignity, then less favourable treatment on the basis of age which does not involve dignitary harm or express contempt will be more readily justified.[45]

In addition to arguments regarding the role of dignity as a foundational concept of equality law in general and age discrimination in particular, dignity has been used in a very specific way in legal debates over retirement. One of the justifications for imposing mandatory retirement in the EU case law has been that retirement can help avoid the indignity that can otherwise occur when disciplinary processes are triggered to force out older workers on the basis of poor performance or incapacity. For example, in *Rosenbladt*[46] the CJEU accepted as legitimate the aim of avoiding dismissal of older workers because 'they are no longer capable of working, which may be humiliating for those who have reached an advanced age.' Similarly, in *Hörnfeldt v Meddelande*[47] the CJEU confirmed as legitimate the aim of avoiding 'a situation in which

---

43 K. Karst, 'The Coming Crisis Of Work In Constitutional Perspective' [1997] Cornell LR 523, 532.

44 This argument is made on the assumption that any retirement policy is imposed in order to ensure the turnover of employment from the older to the younger generation, discussed above at page 6.

45 The use of this argument in the Canadian case law is discussed below at page 77 ff.

46 *Rosenbladt -v- Ollerking Gebaudereinigungsges.mbH* C-45/09 at para 43.

47 Case C-141/11 Judgment of the CJEU 5 July 2012.

employment contracts are terminated in situations which are humiliating for elderly workers'.[48] In effect, the Court has accepted retirement as a gentler form of performance management, allowing careers to end naturally, rather than in humiliating disciplinary processes.

Whilst it was argued above that dignity arguments should not automatically lead to the eradication of retirement, it is equally plain that dignity should not be used to justify retirement in this way. This particular use of dignity makes assumptions that performance deteriorates with age, and that older workers may need help in recognizing this. It thus relies on stereotypes not only about declining capability but also about reduced insight into one's abilities, just the sort of prejudicial assumptions that the law on age discrimination is designed to combat.

The role of dignity in age discrimination is thus more complex than might at first seem. First, the concept of dignity itself can be contested and contradictory. For example, attempts to avoid humiliation for older workers by enforcing retirement may be framed as dignity claims, but are themselves imbued with aged based stereotypes and are instead antithetical to a dignity based approach. Second, dignity arguments can be used on both sides in cases of differential treatment on the basis of age. On the one hand, dignity based arguments can overcome difficulties which might otherwise arise in relation to discrimination claims, for example in finding the correct comparator. A dignity based approach allows a court to be sensitive to the wrongs that are wrought by stereotype and disrespect attached to different age groups. On the other hand, age claims may at the same time be weakened when based on dignity; to the extent that less favourable treatment is based not on contempt or stigma but on more neutral economic grounds, it might be justified.

In effect, dignity is a plastic concept, open to many interpretations and able to be deployed in its various guises on both sides of any debate. Thus although reliance on dignity may help frame our understanding of age discrimination in some respects, if age equality law is framed only as a dignity based right, our understanding of its compass will remain incomplete.

Stigma

Fredman suggests that, rather than relying on the idea of dignity, it may be helpful to disaggregate the social aims of equality law, by focusing instead on developing 'recognition' and eradicating stigma and stereotype. Such ideas are based on the same foundational ideas around human dignity but they give more concrete content to what may otherwise be a somewhat opaque concept.

48 At para 34.

One alternative reading of equality law, which may enhance our understanding of age discrimination, is to conceptualise discrimination as concerned with addressing stigma.[49] Solanke uses the concept of stigma to better understand when characteristics should be protected from discrimination, proposing that equality law should aim to remove the stigma that attaches to particular characteristics and results in disapproval and social opprobrium or contempt. She argues that stigma is not only the result of individual face to face social processes, but can be institutional and structural, with roots in cultural practices and social policies. Applied in the context of age, discrimination experienced by both young and older workers can be understood as, at times, stigmatic. In terms of negative stereotypes,[50] older workers can be stereotyped as less able to adapt to new ways of working, unlikely to have the stamina to maintain intensive levels of work, and unwilling to work for younger managers. Young people, for example 'millennials,'[51] are often stereotyped as unreliable, unable to take direction and lacking in institutional loyalty.[52] Whilst much of the less favourable treatment experienced on the basis of age is based on stereotype, age inequality also infiltrates many labour market practices and social policies, with retirement and age related pay being the most direct examples. To the extent that these policies reflect unequal social power, they can be understood to reflect the stigma attached to age.

But as Solanke shows, stigma goes beyond relying on stereotypes as it does not require any cognitive response from the individual. It can be 'low, unobtrusive and genteel in its effect.'[53] It may appear to be based on kindness but can result in shunning people, leading to social exclusion. In the context of age discrimination this 'genteel' or 'kind' but nonetheless discriminatory treatment can be seen in the use of 'dignity' arguments to justify retirement. This supposedly avoids creating a humiliating environment at work, yet such treatment

---

49 See I. Solanke, *Discrimination as Stigma: A Theory of Anti-Discrimination Law* (2017, Hart Publishing, Oxford).

50 See for example, S. Bisom-Rapp and M. Sargeant, 'Diverging Doctrine, Converging Outcomes: Evaluating Age Discrimination Law in the United Kingdom and the United States' (2013) 44 *Loyola University Chicago Law Journal* 717 available at http://ssrn.com/abstract=2154327.

51 Those born between 1980 and 2000.

52 See for example, PWC report 'Millennials at work Reshaping the workplace' available at https://www.pwc.com/m1/en/services/consulting/documents/millennials-at-work.pdf (accessed 27 November 2017).

53 I. Solanke, *Discrimination as Stigma: A Theory of Anti-Discrimination Law* (2017, Hart Publishing, Oxford), quoting R.A. Pinker, Social Theory and Social Policy (London, Heinemann 1971).

labels older workers as having reduced capacity and results in the removal from older workers of the economic and social benefits of work, resulting in reduced welfare and increased isolation of older people. Understanding discrimination as addressing stigma can be helpful in the context of age, as it helps draw attention to some forms of discrimination that could otherwise be hidden. Thus in the context of age equality, differential treatment on the basis of age needs to be examined closely to ensure that it is not overtly or unobtrusively stigmatic.

But equally, as with the argument based on dignity, the idea that discrimination should aim to eradicate stigma can cut both ways. Unlike the other grounds of discrimination, in the case of age discrimination, the economic dimension to age equality creates a number of scenarios in which it may be argued that age based treatment is not the result of stigma or stereotype. It may be that where differential treatment does not impose stigma on the group, it will be more readily justified.

Disadvantage

An alternative aim of equality is, in Arneson's words, 'to promote better lives for people, with good quality of life fairly distributed, and fairness understood as tilting towards the worse off.'[54] Such an approach sees the wrong of discrimination as being in the way it causes disadvantage, rather than in terms of expressive harm. One of the consequences of aiming at redressing disadvantage, or more radically, redistributing wealth, is that it allows for asymmetric protection, focussed on improving the lot of the disadvantaged group or person, rather than on treating both parties in the same way.

Tackling disadvantage goes beyond economic disadvantage, and can be understood to include differential access, caused by membership of a protected group, to enjoyment of the more general good of human flourishing.[55] Thus the disadvantage may not only be reduced economic opportunities such as access to work, but also can caused by reductions in self-esteem. In effect, concepts such as stigma and dignity can thus be viewed through a lens of disadvantage, rather than as separate aims of equality.

As was seen in relation to dignity and stigma, there are correlations between age and a level of disadvantage in terms of an ability to live a flourishing life, both for older and younger people;[56] and the link between economic

---

54 R. Arneson, 'Discrimination, Disparate Impact and Theories of Justice' in D. Hellman and S. Moreau, *Philosophical Foundations of Discrimination Law* (Oxford, OUP, 2013).

55 T. Khaitan, *A Theory of Discrimination Law* (Oxford, OUP, 2015).

56 See further A.L. Goldman, 'Age Discrimination Law—A Perspective from the USA' in F. Hendrickx (ed.) *Active Ageing and Labour Law* (2012, Intersentia, Cambridge).

disadvantage and age was identified above, under the economic dimension. For example, there is some correlation between age and economic disadvantage, with high rates of under- and unemployment for young people leading to reduced incomes, and increased longevity leading to poverty in old age.[57] However, the correlation of poverty with older ages is not direct. Indeed, some over-65s enjoy better financial status not only than those of other age groups but better financial status than later generations are ever likely to enjoy. Thus, it cannot be assumed than higher levels of wealth enjoyed towards the end of life are an inevitable product of changes over a life time, and thus justified because they are available to all in turn.

Moreover, as suggested above, not all disbenefits that may be linked to age are stigmatic or infringe dignity. Some merely reflect the economic dimensions of age equality, and are aimed to avoid some of the repercussions of a labour market which embeds age into its structures, such as redundancy schemes and pay scales. Indeed, disadvantage is usually understood to include the historic and systemic disadvantages suffered by groups, often based on historically entrenched stigma. In the context of age, this may be where the fact that individuals' ages are subject to change gains purchase within the aims of non-discrimination law, because the experience of the group and of the individual do not correspond directly.

Stereotypes based on age can act to the detriment of older workers. Such stereotypes are long standing, and the resulting detriment can be understood to be systemic and historic; it can be viewed as group disadvantage because it is suffered by older workers because of their membership of the category of 'older workers'. However, each individual claimant will not have experienced disadvantage in a systemic way, as they will have had periods of their lives when they were not subject to the detriment.[58] This is in contrast to other protected groups whose group and individual experiences of disadvantage is constant and can therefore be understood to be systemic. The application of concepts such as systemic or historic as multipliers of disadvantage is thus problematic in the case of age.[59]

57 See Income Poverty in Old Age: An Emerging Development Priority, UN Department of Economic and Social Affairs, Programme on Ageing, available at: http://www.un.org/esa/socdev/ageing/documents/PovertyIssuePaperAgeing.pdf accessed 30/10/17.

58 See the discussion of the complete life view of equality in R. Horton, 'Justifying Age Discrimination in the EU' in U. Belavusau and K. Henrard, *EU Anti-Discrimination Law beyond Gender* (Hart Publishing, Oxford, 2018).

59 E. Pontz, 'What a difference ADEA makes: why disparate impact theory should not apply to Age Discrimination Act' (1995–6) 74 NCL Rev 267.

In effect, correctly identifying where disadvantage on grounds of age arises creates a constant challenge where equality law is based on the aim of redressing disadvantage, with an associated danger that action that aims to tackle disadvantage will be colonised by the more advantaged members of the group.[60] In the context of age, this can be seen in the increased use of age equality laws by older white men in the US, noted above.[61]

However, the fact that disadvantage is not directly correlated to age does not mean that equality law should not direct its attention to redressing disadvantage where there is evidence that it is age-based. It is merely to note that care needs to be taken when using disadvantage in the context of age equality, as age cannot be used as an accurate proxy for disadvantage.

Moreover, even where a correlation can be seen between economic disadvantage and age, it is not clear how much weight it should be given when it is the result of individual circumstances including past choices, rather than systemic disadvantage suffered throughout life, as with other protected characteristics. Sometimes, age related disadvantage will be connected to systemic disadvantage: for example, as was pointed out above, some women may suffer an economic disadvantage if they have taken time out from work to bring up children; or they may have reached the upper levels of promotion fairly late on in their careers, meaning that they have not had a fair 'crack at the whip' when it comes to career progression. Yet, there will be cases where an individual suffers economic detriment and poor financial security for reasons that give rise to less concern. For example, a person may lack pension provision because they cashed in their pension funds to buy a car,[62] or to spend on lavish holidays; or conditions may arise that are not chosen, but which are not connected to protected characteristics, such as family breakdown, which can have serious negative impacts on family finances. It would clearly be invidious for employers or courts to assess such personal circumstances when assessing whether discrimination can be justified, but equally it may be inadequate to simply

60 L. Barmes, Equality Law and Experimentation: The Positive Action Challenge (2009) 68 CLJ 623.

61 G. Rutherglen, 'From Race to Age: the Expanding Scope of Employment Discrimination Law (1995) 24(2). *The Journal of Legal Studies* 491; JN Lahey, International Comparison of Age Discrimination Laws (2010) 32 (6) *Res Aging* 679.

62 See for example, the comment by the UK pensions minister who said "If people do get a Lamborghini, and end up on the state pension, the state is much less concerned about that, and that is their choice", following a change in UK law from 2015 in which people reaching retirement age can use pension pots however they want rather than having to buy a guaranteed annual income http://www.bbc.co.uk/news/uk-politics-26649162 (accessed 4 December 2017).

assume that any economic disadvantage faced by an older person should be 'compensated' by allowing the older worker's interests to be given priority over the interests of younger workers. None of this is to say that the law should not aim to redress some of the disadvantages faced by older workers, it is merely to note that the issue is complex and contains internal contradictions. As a result, while disadvantage may play a useful role as part of a matrix of concerns to which non-discrimination law should have regard, it should not be assumed to take priority over other aims for discrimination law.[63]

Inclusion

A further aim for equality law is that of social inclusion and participation in society, both political participation and inclusion in community and society more generally.[64] The idea of social inclusion as an additional aim for equality is suggested by Collins,[65] for whom the idea has a clear redistributive purpose. In Collins' view, a focus on social inclusion can help overcome some of the problems, identified above, with equality law having as its aim the preservation of dignity or eradication of disadvantage. Collins' focus on social inclusion moves away from a concern with equalising treatment, and aims instead to meet minimum levels of wellbeing for all. Wellbeing in this context extends beyond economic and physical wellbeing, to include an ability to engage meaningfully in social life, including public life and work. As with the focus on stigma and dignity, the concept involves extending our understanding of the wrongs of age discrimination beyond the economic, but nonetheless, the focus remains on structural and systemic disadvantage.[66] The social inclusion model focusses both on positive action to achieve greater distributive justice, but also encourages the participation of minority groups in civic life, so that their voice within the community can become stronger, thereby reducing their marginalisation. Both Fraser[67] and Fredman[68] advocate full participation in society as an aim of equality, as a mechanism for increasing social justice. They suggest

63 See E. Anderson, 'What is the point of Equality?' (1999) 109(2) *Ethics* 287 on the problems for equality law when effectively based on 'luck egalitarianism'.

64 S. Fredman, 'Substantive Equality Revisited' (2016) 14(3) International Journal of Constitutional Law 712.

65 H. Collins, 'Discrimination, Equality and Social Inclusion' (2003) 66 *MLR* 16.

66 Applied in the context of age, this leads Collins to focus his concern on those over 55 and under 22 as these are the groups that suffer from structural and systemic disadvantage.

67 N. Fraser, 'From Redistribution to Recognition? Dilemmas of Justice in a 'Post-Socialist' Age' (1995) New Left Review 1/212 68.

68 S. Fredman, 'Substantive Equality Revisited' (2016) 14(3) International Journal of Constitutional Law 712.

that fuller and more substantive conceptions of equality would involve working to increase participation in decision making by members of out-groups. This can include greater participation in the political sphere, to ensure that the voice of marginalised groups is properly heard in our democratic processes. Anderson reaches similar conclusions in her review of the aims of equality, with her suggestion that the focus of non-discrimination should be on institutional arrangements that generate people's opportunities rather than on creating an even distribution of goods.[69]

Applying such arguments in the context of age leads yet again to a degree of contradiction. On the one hand, the political voice of some older and younger people, especially those experiencing poverty and social disadvantage caused by stigma and stereotyping may be excluded from our democratic processes if they lack the confidence or self-esteem to participate. On the other hand, there is plenty of evidence from voting patterns that older people as a group do not lack voice in the political process.[70] Indeed, it can be argued that their voice is disproportionate in the democratic process, with the result that policy is often directed towards serving the interests of older voters. This suggests that at least in terms of democratic processes, age does not correlate with a lack of participation in political terms.

Thus, to the extent that age can lead to marginalisation either in terms of participation directly in politics or in wider processes of social life, inclusion can provide a useful dimension of equality law. Our understanding of equality can be helpfully expanded by an appreciation that where stereotypical or stigmatic assumptions based on age lead individuals to be excluded from work, broader social exclusion will occur. However, there is some danger is assuming that age is a reliable proxy for marginalisation, so while a focus on inclusion is useful to provide a broad understanding of the wrongs of discrimination, it should be used with caution in relation to age, and with due regard for the varied contexts in which it operates.

---

69 E. Anderson, 'What is the point of equality?' (1999) 109(2) Ethics 287.

70 In the USA, see https://www.census.gov/data/tables/time-series/demo/voting-and-registration/p20-580.html; for the UK see https://yougov.co.uk/news/2017/06/13/how-britain-voted-2017-general-election/ See also A. Solijonov, *Voter Turnout Trends around the World* (2016) International IDEA, Stockholm) who concludes "Age is one of the most important factors to affect voter turnout. Youth voter apathy is a primary source of concern in many countries. The findings of the World Value Survey research conducted between 2010 and 2014 show significant differences in voter turnout between people aged 25 or under and those aged 26 or over. The research covered 59 countries representing all the regions of the world." Available at https://www.idea.int/sites/default/files/publications/voter-turnout-trends-around-the-world.pdf (accessed 5 Dec 2017).

Accommodation

Fredman's fourth dimensional principle of equality is to 'respect and accommodate difference, removing the detriment but not the difference itself', which involves changing existing social structures to accommodate difference, rather than requiring everyone to conform to the dominant norm.[71] Fredman argues that accommodation, a concept used in the context of disability discrimination, can usefully be incorporated into our understanding of equality on other grounds, with its emphasis on addressing structures which give rise to disadvantage, whether that is in terms of the physical structures of workplaces, or work rules and other practices that may place groups at a disadvantage. Examples may be requirements to work full time, which may disadvantage parents, or requirements to wear particular clothing, which may be to the detriment of religious minorities. Accommodation can refer to general structural change, or more narrowly to the creation of exceptions for individuals leaving the general rule untouched.[72]

Applied in the context of age, the idea that general structures could be changed to ameliorate the position of older or younger workers is attractive. For example, dismantling age dependent structures may be helpful where they are based on stereotypical assumptions, such as wage structures which assume that younger worker's financial needs are less than those of older workers, and redeployment schemes which assume that younger workers will not have dependants, assuming that they are can easily be mobile. However, more broadly, courts have been wary of introducing deeper structural change in relation to age. Age related rules are firmly embedded not only within the workplace, but also social security rules and other social structures. This makes creating comprehensive change extremely complex. Given the varied aspects of age equality, including economic dimensions and the contradictions within the different social dimensions, it is perhaps understandable that courts have been wary of requiring fundamental structural changes to employment, pension and other economic arrangements as a method of addressing age discrimination.[73]

Despite the reluctance of courts to require generalised and systemic change to labour market structures in response to age discrimination, a more individualised exception based approach to accommodation may be of use in the

---

71 S. Fredman, 'Substantive Equality Revisited' (2016) 14(3) International Journal of Constitutional Law 712, at p. 733.

72 Ibid. at p. 733.

73 See M. Freedland and L. Vickers, 'Age Discrimination and EU labour rights law' in A. Bogg, C. Costello and A. Davies (eds), *A Research Handbook on EU Labour* Law (Cheltenham, Edward Elgar, 2016).

context of age, akin to the duty of reasonable accommodation or reasonable adjustment that applies in the case of disability discrimination. Such an approach would require employers to justify any refusal to make individual adaptations to workplace rules which are needed to allow younger people or older people to access employment more easily. A number of examples of accommodation can be found in the UK. For example, the system for assessing the quality of research in UK higher education institutions, the Research Excellence Framework,[74] uses certain metrics to measure research output. The metrics are adapted to allow early career researchers to submit fewer outputs, to take into account of the fact that they have had less time to produce research. While not directly linked to age, this adjustment is largely of benefit to younger academics. Older workers may be accommodated by allowing them to continue to progress careers even if they lack qualifications which are later introduced for new recruits.[75] Alternatively, within the National Health Service, common requests for accommodation from older workers are for flexible working, or reduced night-working.[76]

An individualised based approach to accommodation allows for exceptions to be made to adapt work structures to the needs of individuals. Such an approach helps address the individualised experience of inequality, and to that extent helps achieve the broader social aims of equality. Moreover, the language of reasonable accommodation as applied to age can help not only to address more localised concerns, but also the intersection between age equality and other grounds, particularly disability discrimination. However, this exception based approach stops short of addressing underlying causes of age inequality, and thus can be understood as a limited aim for age equality laws.

Intersectionality

The discussion above demonstrates that there are inherent contradictions both within and between the varied aspects of the social dimension to age equality. Age has a strong correlation with a number of negative social outcomes, as well as being linked to forms of economic disadvantage, and yet

74 For information see http://www.ref.ac.uk/ (accessed 6 December 2017).

75 See *Homer v Chief Constable of West Yorkshire* [2012] UKSC 15, and the final Employment Tribunal decision at *Homer v Chief Constable of West Yorkshire Police* ET/1803238/2007.

76 N. Johnson and S. Manfredi, 'Older Workers in the Nursing and Midwifery Profession' in S. Manfredi and L. Vickers (ed.), *Challenges of Active Ageing: Equality Law and the Workplace*, Palgrave Macmillan UK (2016).

the traditional justifications for non-discrimination laws do not apply in a straightforward manner: the benefits and disadvantages experienced over the life course mean that it is not always clear who is the disadvantaged group; 'age' does not capture a discrete group that has been excluded from majoritarian political processes; and age is not always used in ways that infer stigma or undermine dignity.

One way to make the links between age and economic or social disbenefits clearer is to understand age equality in intersectional terms.[77] Once the connections between age and other protected characteristics are understood, the case for protection against age discrimination strengthens.

The term intersectionality was used by Crenshaw to identify the particular oppressions suffered by black women by virtue of being both black and women,[78] although its recognition can be traced earlier to activists such as Sojourner Truth.[79] Intersectionality goes beyond the recognition of the cumulative effect and mutual reinforcement of multiple discrimination, when individuals are disadvantaged by two or more of the protected characteristics at the same time. Instead, it recognises the 'intersectional experience as a product of the intermeshing, or fusion, of two or more separate forms of oppression, rather than just simultaneous or parallel occurrences of these oppressions.'[80]

An understanding of age equality through the lens of intersectionality helps identify gaps in the legal protection afforded to age, as well as creating additional impetus for tackling age discrimination. For example, the different social aims of age equality are more pressing once their intersection with other grounds is recognised: while there is a correlation between poverty and older age, it is significantly more common for older women to experience poverty

77 See J. Fudge and A. Zbyszewska, 'An Intersectional Approach to Age Discrimination' in A. Numhauser-Henning and M. Rönnmar (eds), *Age Discrimination and Labour Law: Comparative and Conceptual Perspectives in the EU and Beyond* (Kluwer, The Netherlands, 2015).

78 K. Crenshaw, 'Demarginalizing the Intersection of Race and Sex: A Black Feminist Critique of Antidiscrimination Doctrine, Feminist Theory, and Antiracist Politics', University of Chicago Legal Forum, 1989, 139.

79 I. Solanke, *Discrimination as Stigma: A Theory of Anti-Discrimination Law* (2017, Hart Publishing, Oxford), 142.

80 J.J. Votinius, 'Intersectionality as a Tool for Analysing Labour Law' in S. Manfredi and L. Vickers (ed.), *Challenges of Active Ageing: Equality Law and the Workplace*, Palgrave Macmillan UK (2016).

than older men, largely due to a significant gap in pension provision;[81] and additional stigma and negative stereotypes are directed at older women.[82]

The intersections of age with gender are well established.[83] Votinius[84] identifies particular disadvantages experienced by older women: first, she shows that the ageing of the population has a greater impact on women as they are more likely to have been already disadvantaged in the workplace due to sex discrimination; this means that justifications for unequal treatment on the basis of age may be inapt, such as the 'fair innings' argument that suggests that older workers should give way to younger workers once a predetermined age is reached. The justification that is usually offered for this position is that older workers have already enjoyed the benefits of a full working life. But of course, women are likely to be disproportionately represented among those who have not, due to the higher likelihood that they will have interrupted their careers for child or elder care related reasons. In similar vein, stereotypes of age and gender may differ: women are viewed as 'old' from a younger age, older women are seen as less competent, intelligent or wise then older men; as well as being viewed as more nurturing and sensitive, referencing grandmotherly stereotypes.[85] In addition, the combination of age and gender may exacerbate existing stereotypes. For example, stereotypes about older people being reluctant to adopt new technology may be stronger for women, given that women are also stereotyped as being less technically proficient than men.[86]

---

81 See S. Fredman, *Intersectional Discrimination in EU Gender Equality and Non-Discrimination* (2016, European Commission, Brussels) and *Rights, jobs and social security: New visions for older women and men* http://www.ilo.org/gender/Events/Campaign2008-2009/WCMS_098840/lang--en/index.htm.

82 See for example campaigns over the scarcity of roles for older women in the media (e.g. Geena Davis Institute on Gender in Media; and *O'Reilly -v- BBC and others*, London Central Employment Tribunal, case number 22004223/2010).

83 S. Bisom-Rapp and M. Sargeant, 'It's Complicated: Age, Gender, and Lifetime Discrimination against Working Women—the United States and the U.K. as Examples' (2014) 22 Elder L.J. 1.

84 J.J. Votinius, 'Intersectionality as a Tool for Analysing Labour Law' in Manfredi S, Vickers L (ed.), *Challenges of Active Ageing: Equality Law and the Workplace*, Palgrave Macmillan UK (2016).

85 S.M. Saldarriaga, 'Flaming Fifties and beyond: An International Comparison of Age Discrimination Laws and How the United States Could Improve the Laws for Elderly Women', (2017) 25 *Elder L.J.* 101.

86 J.J. Votinius, 'Intersectionality as a Tool for Analysing Labour Law' in S. Manfredi and L. Vickers (ed.), *Challenges of Active Ageing: Equality Law and the Workplace*, Palgrave Macmillan UK (2016), at 109.

Another key intersection is between age and disability.[87] Not only do rates of disability increase with age, but also many of the common requests that older workers make for accommodation or adjustment are very similar to requests that would otherwise be understood as disability claims if made by younger workers. For example, requests to avoid some of the peaks of intensive or unsocial working hours, or to allow sufficient recovery time following such work schedules could be understood as either claims based on disability, or where made by older workers, claims based on age. As well as clear intersections between age and disability, additional intersections can be found between disability, age and gender. For example, older women have consistently been found to have higher prevalence of disability than men of the same age, due to surviving longer after disabilities arise.[88] Age intersects with other grounds in relation to ethnic origin and sexual orientation too,[89] with young ethnic minority people suffering discriminatory treatment on grounds of ethnic minority or immigration status.[90]

Whilst intersectionality largely creates additional impetus for tackling age equality, it may at times create additional forms of justification for age discrimination. For example, after the abolition of mandatory retirement in the UK, Oxford University retained its use of retirement for academic staff. One of its justifications is to help the university achieve greater diversity across its staffing, 'noting that recent recruits are more diverse than the composition of the existing workforce, especially amongst the older age groups of the existing workforce.'[91]

---

87 Identified as one of the most common combinations of equality grounds in M. Hudson, ACAS Research Paper 01/12: The experience of discrimination on multiple grounds, 2012, available at: http://www.acas.org.uk/media/pdf/0/3/0112_Multidiscrim_Hudson-accessible-version-Apr-2012.pdf. (accessed 8 December 2017).

88 J.M. Guralnik, S.G. Leveille et al. 'The impact of disability in older women' (1997) 52(3) J Am Med Women's Assoc. 113.

89 S. Fredman, *Intersectional Discrimination in EU Gender Equality and Non-Discrimination* (2016, European Commission, Brussels).

90 FRA EU-MIDIS Data in Focus Report (2010), Multiple Discrimination cited by S. Fredman, *Intersectional Discrimination in EU Gender Equality and Non-Discrimination* (2016, European Commission, Brussels).

91 See the aims of the Oxford University Employer Justified Retirement Age, available at https://www.admin.ox.ac.uk/personnel/end/retirement/acrelretire8+/erjaaims/ (accessed 8 December 2017). See also C. Barnard and S. Deakin, *Age Discrimination and Labour Law in the UK: Managing Ageing* in A. Numhauser-Henning and M. Rönnmar (eds), *Age Discrimination and Labour Law: Comparative and Conceptual Perspectives in the EU and Beyond* (Kluwer, The Netherlands, 2015).

Legal systems differ in the extent to which they recognise the intersectional dimension to discrimination.[92] Courts have been slow to formally recognise the more intermeshed forms of intersectional harm caused by discrimination, although there are some exceptions where courts have recognised that discrimination may arise from the intersection of different grounds.[93]

More limited recognition of intersectionality can be seen in the recognition by some states of multiple discrimination claims. However, even in this simpler form of adding together more than one type of discrimination the position varies. For example within the Europe, a variety of practices exist: multiple discrimination is explicitly recognized in Greece[94] and Bulgaria;[95] the UK[96] and the Netherlands do not explicitly recognise multiple discrimination; and in Romania[97] and Austria,[98] the fact that discrimination has occurred on more than one ground can give grounds for additional damages.

Broad recognition of intersectional discrimination thus remains to be seen on the legal stage, but the concept of intersectionality is of significance to both the social and economic dimensions of equality law, and should enrich our understanding of the aims of equality law on the grounds of age.

Conclusion

The case for legal protection against age discrimination in the employment sphere is clear: age discrimination can give rise to expressive and economic harms. Disadvantageous treatment of older and younger workers has a number of outcomes including difficulties for older and young people in accessing work; detrimental treatment in work though differential pay; lack of career progression due to the use of stereotypes; and the premature ending of careers through age related redundancy schemes or compulsory retirement.

---

92 B. Smith, *Intersectional Discrimination and Substantive Equality: A Comparative and Theoretical Perspective* (2016) 16 The Equal Rights Review 73.

93 See for example, *Law v Canada* [1999] 1 SCR 497.

94 Greece, Equal Treatment Law 4443/2016, Article 2(2)(g).

95 Bulgaria, Protection against Discrimination Act, Additional Provisions, § 1.11.

96 Although the Equality Act 2010 contains a provision prohibiting discrimination because of a combination of two protected characteristics, this provision has not been brought into force.

97 Romania, Anti-discrimination Law, Article 2(6): 'Any distinction, exclusion, restriction or preference based on two or more of the criteria foreseen in para. 1 shall constitute an aggravating circumstance in establishing responsibility for a minor offence, unless one or more of its components is not subject to criminal law'.

98 Austria, Federal-Equal Treatment Act, Para. 19a and Equal Treatment Act, Paras. 12/13, 26/13, and 51/10.

However, the strongly detrimental impact of age discrimination only tells half the story, as age also plays a strong role in the structures of the employment relationship, at times aiming to address other forms of injustice, such as intergenerational justice whereby older workers may be expected to retire to make way for a younger, and at times more diverse workforce.[99]

The interaction between the social and economic dimensions of age equality can be seen in particular in the case of retirement. In the following section, retirement serves as a case study of the various ways in which different aspects of age equality intersect, and as illustration of the contradictions that courts face when required to assess whether compulsory retirement can be justified.

The Intersection of the Economic and Social: The Case of Retirement

The case for abolishing compulsory retirement can be made on both economic and social justice grounds. Increasing longevity and the consequent difficulties facing states in maintaining pension provision has led to calls for extended working lives, a clear obstacle to the achievement of which is the practice of compulsory retirement. Added to this forceful economic argument against compulsory retirement is a rights based argument which sees the practice as discriminatory: it amounts to an affront to individual dignity, particularly as the treatment is often based on stereotypical assumptions about capacity reducing with age.[100]

The case against retirement is simple and forceful, and is to be taken seriously. However, it is not unassailable and it is arguable that compulsory retirement can, at times, be justified. First, as suggested above, retirement may be justified when viewed as part of a protective labour market structure which provides support for workers throughout their careers, culminating in provision of an adequate pension. Some also justify compulsory retirement using the notions of a 'fair innings' or complete life view of age equality, as well as on the basis of intergenerational justice referred to above.[101] The argument is that

99 See the aims of the Oxford University Employer Justified Retirement Age, available at https://www.admin.ox.ac.uk/personnel/end/retirement/acrelretire8+/erjaaims/ (accessed 8 December 2017). See also C. Barnard and S. Deakin, *Age Discrimination and Labour Law in the UK: Managing Ageing* in A. Numhauser-Henning and M. Rönnmar (eds), *Age Discrimination and Labour Law: Comparative and Conceptual Perspectives in the EU and Beyond* (Kluwer, The Netherlands, 2015).

100 J. Grimley Evans, Age discrimination: Implications of the Ageing Process' in S. Fredman and S. Spencer, *Age as an Equality Issue: Legal and Policy Perspectives* (Hart Publishing, Oxford, 2003).

101 At page 6.

it is acceptable to expect older workers to make way for younger workers once a particular age is reached. The fair innings argument assumes that fairness should be viewed over a life time; that older workers who might otherwise be understood to be disadvantaged by any such requirement, have in fact enjoyed the same benefits in their youth. Such a view is associated with a broad social policy agenda of intergenerational fairness, achieved through the sharing of jobs between generations.

Although relied on by some courts in age discrimination cases,[102] the 'fair innings' idea has been criticised on the basis that jobs need not be rationed as the number of jobs is not finite.[103] However, although it can be argued that more people working will result in the creation of more jobs, this economic model would seem to be less appropriate at the individual firm or sector levels: for example, although the number of jobs in higher education may not be finite, nonetheless, the number of positions cannot just expand to meet demand for jobs. Thus where senior positions remain occupied by older workers, it remains difficult for younger staff to gain employment or promotion.

Although economic arguments can be deployed to suggest that the notion of a fair innings or intergenerational fairness can justify compulsory retirement, this will only be socially just if the innings have truly been 'fair'. As referred to above in relation to the issue of incremental pay rates in the traditional labour market, some workers will not have had a 'fair innings' for example due to absence for family or health reasons. Equally, the extent to which any innings is fair may depend on where in the labour market the individual is situated, and in practice this can depend on their labour market position. Those who are located in the higher segments of the labour market,[104] such as professionals with a high level of human capital, are likely to have an occupational pension or other savings for their retirement, and so will often have genuine choice as to whether to continue to work or retire. Those in low paid and low skill jobs have fewer options and may not have sufficient pension income to retire comfortably. Thus, even if it is accepted that intergenerational justice may be a legitimate aim, it remains far from clear whether such aims will be sufficient to justify mandatory retirement in any given case.

Moreover, even if the arguments in favour of retirement are accepted, the basic egalitarian case against compulsory retirement, that it amounts to age

---

102 See for example in the UK *Seldon v Clarkson Wright and Jakes* [2012] UKSC 16.

103 S. Fredman, 'The Age of Equality; in S. Fredman and S. Spencer, Age as an Equality Issue: Legal and Policy Perspectives (Oxford, Hart Publishing, 2003) at p. 46.

104 M. Reich, D.M. Gordon and R.C. Edwards, Dual Labour Markets: A Theory of Labour Market Segmentation (1982) 17 J Human Resources 359.

discrimination, remains to be answered. To a degree, these concerns can be met, as the social dimension of age equality is not as robust as it might seem. For example, as discussed above, arguments for age equality based on dignity and disadvantage are weakened when age based differences in treatment are not used as signifiers of contempt for older workers, but are based on the understanding of the job as an economic asset, which should be distributed fairly between the generations in order to address economic disadvantage faced by younger workers.[105] However, the social arguments against differential treatment on the basis of age remain robust, leading difficulty for national courts when determining the outcome of cases involving retirement.

Connecting the Social and Economic

The various dimensions of age equality have been shown to be complex and at times internally contradictory. Changes in demographics mean that age is used as a key category in addressing institutional responses to economic challenges caused by the ageing population. At the same time, age equality also has an individual aspect, in terms of its role in leading to dignitary harm to the individual. In effect, age equality can be understood to have both individual and institutional features.

An additional aspect of the economic dimension to age equality is identified by Somek,[106] who notes that by removing the barriers which can stop people working, equality law acts as a corrective to the neoliberal turn in economics and social policy. In effect, as the workplace increasingly operates within a market framework, it is necessary to remove barriers on the participation of vulnerable groups within the market. Given the increasing flexibilisation of work and the move to more precarious forms of work, the discrimination agenda can thus be understood as a mechanism to soften what might otherwise become a fairly brutal labour market system with little room to accommodate any vulnerability. The assumption is that once the corrective of anti-discrimination law is applied, the market can then be left to operate with minimal further state intervention.[107]

105 S. Manfredi, and L. Vickers, 'Meeting the challenges of active ageing in the workplace: is the abolition of retirement the answer?' *European Labour Law Journal* 4 (4) (2013) 251.

106 A. Somek, *Engineering Equality An Essay on European Anti-Discrimination Law* (OUP, Oxford, 2011).

107 See further S Manfredi and L Vickers, 'Meeting the challenges of active ageing in the workplace: is the abolition of retirement the answer?' (2013) 4(4) *European Labour Law Journal* 251.

Much of the impetus for introducing anti-discrimination laws for age has, indeed, been driven by economic imperatives to increase labour market participation, and it may well be the case that age equality laws result in a bolstering of reliance on a free labour market by removing some of its inefficiencies and inequities. In effect, the broad impact of age discrimination within the labour market provides strong reasons to give effective regard to the economic dimension to equality law as means to create fairer distribution of economic goods.

Nonetheless it also remains the case that the gains of anti-discrimination law are felt well beyond the economic sphere. Whilst economic imperatives may be a major driver of change towards a more age-equal society, the resulting changes have significant non-economic benefits in terms of progress towards a more equal society in broader terms.

Thus, the two dimensions of age equality, the social and the economic need to be seen in tandem. Indeed, it may well be helpful to see the different dimensions as intersectional rather than additive. A full appreciation of the aims of age equality requires more than the addition of the various harms under different headings. Instead, they need to be understood to be interwoven in a more complex manner. On the one hand, the different dimensions sometimes work cumulatively to create additional elements of harm. On the other hand, they can also cut across and undermine each other, leading to justification of differential treatment.

A framework for achieving a legal approach to age equality drawing on the intersection between its social and economic aims, without creating any priority between them, and without merely seeing the two dimensions as additive, is suggested by Fredman's approach to understanding substantive equality. In her 2016 article *Substantive Equality Revisited*,[108] she uses the four-dimensional analytic framework of equality discussed above to better illuminate the nature of inequality, and assist in determining the outcome of cases. Fredman's focus is on the interaction of the different dimensions of equality, using the synergies and synthesis between them to help resolve difficult cases. Thus, she suggests that furthering dignity should not be at the expense of redressing disadvantage; and that affirming identity should be circumscribed by the need to prevent stigma, stereotyping and prejudice.[109] In effect, the different dimensions of equality can be used to buttress one another and better address the weaknesses of each.[110]

---

108 (2016) 14(3) International Journal of Constitutional Law 712.

109 Ibid. at 714.

110 Ibid. at 735.

Such a multi-layered approach can be useful as courts seek to steer a course through the different aspects of age equality, and such an approach is compatible with the legal frameworks based on proportionality.[111] At times, the main aim of the law may be to respond to the economic needs of demographic change. This may justify some structural changes to facilitate greater participation in work by older or younger workers. At other times, the purpose of age discrimination law may be to address dignitary and stigma harms, such as where individuals are harassed or subjected to other detriments due to age related stereotyping. Accepting a range of aims and purposes for age discrimination law, in recognition of the varied dimensions of age inequality, should lead to nuanced and flexible legal responses.

Of course, the use of a multi-dimensional approach to age equality cannot resolve the many contradictions and complexities raised above in the discussion of the social, economic and structural aspects of age equality. Indeed, there are times when the different dimensions do not result in the buttressing or strengthening of protection against age discrimination, but rather the different dimensions may explain and justify limits placed on non-discrimination. For example, despite the fact that the dignity dimensions to age equality may suggest that differential treatment on the basis of age should be unlawful, the economic dimension may lead to a different conclusion in the case of retirement, or age based wage structures. Even here though, the position is not clear cut: intersectional aspects of such decisions can play a role, even though this role may lead to some contradictory results. In the case of retirement an intersectional approach may reveal that retirement can create particular hardship for women who have built up insufficient pension income; but equally, an intersectional approach may suggest that retirement can be justified if it is used to create a more diverse workforce.[112]

The use of a multi-dimensional approach to resolving cases of age discrimination is thus unlikely to lead to conclusive answers on how to reconcile the various conflicting interests in play. Instead, recognition of the different

111 D. Schiek, 'Proportionality in Age Discrimination Cases: Towards a Model Suitable for Socially Embedded Rights' in A. Numhauser-Henning and M. Rönnmar (eds), *Age Discrimination and Labour Law: Comparative and Conceptual Perspectives in the EU and Beyond* (Kluwer, The Netherlands, 2015).

112 See the aims of the Oxford University Employer Justified Retirement Age, available at https://www.admin.ox.ac.uk/personnel/end/retirement/acrelretire8+/erjaaims/ (accessed 8 December 2017). See also C. Barnard and S. Deakin, *Age Discrimination and Labour Law in the UK: Managing Ageing* in A. Numhauser-Henning and M. Rönnmar (eds), *Age Discrimination and Labour Law: Comparative and Conceptual Perspectives in the EU and Beyond* (Kluwer, The Netherlands, 2015).

dimensions of age equality creates a set of evaluative criteria for determining the proper parameters of laws upholding or promoting age equality. The approaches of courts in a range of jurisdictions will be explored in the next chapters in order to identify the extent to which the difficulties courts face in age discrimination cases can be understood as caused by the existence of overlapping and competing economic and social aspects of age equality.

Part 2: Comparative Study

Having examined the multi-faceted challenges facing courts in approaching age equality, this part turns to consider the law in a number of states regarding the prohibition of age discrimination. The study aims to cover the law of the global north and south, but the focus is largely on states where the law has developed in more detail. A number of states such as India, Japan, China Egypt and Nigeria have no generalised protection against age discrimination, although non-legal measures may address age equality.[113]

The law of the various states is first described in general terms. Attention is then focused on discrimination against younger workers, discrimination against older workers in general, and any the special treatment of retirement.

International Standards

Age is not an enumerated ground of equality in the Universal Declaration of Human Rights, nor is there any dedicated international treaty for the eradication of age discrimination. However, to the extent that age discrimination may include elements of intersectional discrimination, international conventions such as the Convention for the Elimination of Discrimination against Women may be of relevance. Some international human rights instruments include references to age in their lists of discrimination, such as the International Convention on the Protection of All Migrant Workers and Members of Their Families and the Convention on the Rights of Persons with Disabilities. In addition, where international conventions include clauses prohibiting

113 See www.agdiscrimination.info for information about age discrimination laws in a wide range of states. See also chapters on individual states in A. Numhauser-Henning and M. Rönnmar (eds), *Age Discrimination and Labour Law: Comparative and Conceptual Perspectives in the EU and Beyond* (Kluwer, The Netherlands, 2015).

discrimination on a number of grounds including 'other status', age has been recognised as included.[114]

A number of non-binding political instruments have been developed to address the disadvantage experienced by both older and younger people: for example, the Vienna International Plan of Action on Ageing was adopted at the World Assembly on Ageing in 1982, followed by the 1991 United Nations Principles for Older Persons, the 1992 Global Targets on Ageing for the Year 2001 and the 1992 Proclamation on Ageing. The Political Declaration and the Madrid International Plan of Action on Ageing, 2002, was adopted at the Second World Assembly on Ageing, and endorsed by the General Assembly.[115] In 2010 the Open-Ended Working Group on Ageing was established by the UN General Assembly, to identify possible gaps in the existing international framework of the human rights of older persons and how best to address them.

Although not directly enforceable, such policy instruments may be of use to courts in interpreting and applying the law in cases of age discrimination. However, overall, in terms of the fundamental rights legal regime, age equality does not directly feature in the framework of international human rights protection.[116]

Despite the absence of an international treaty prohibiting age discrimination, it is directly prohibited under regional legal frameworks such as within the EU legal system, discussed next.

The EU Legal Framework on Age Discrimination

The first step in prohibiting age discrimination in the EU was the introduction in 1997[117] of a new Article 6a to the Treaty on European Union, permitting the EU to take appropriate action to combat discrimination on a number of grounds including age. The resulting Equal Treatment Framework Directive 2000/78/EC included provisions related to age, and is considered below.

---

114 E.g. Article 26 ICCPR. C. O'Cinneide, 'Constitutional and Fundamental Rights Aspects of Age Discrimination' in A. Numhauser-Henning and M. Rönnmar (eds), *Age Discrimination and Labour Law: Comparative and Conceptual Perspectives in the EU and Beyond* (Kluwer, The Netherlands, 2015).

115 See Report of the Secretary-General, Follow-up to the Second World Assembly on Ageing, Sixty-sixth session, 22 July 2011 Available at https://documents-dds-ny.un.org/doc/UNDOC/GEN/N11/428/83/PDF/N1142883.pdf?OpenElement (accessed 13 December 17).

116 C. O'Cinneide, 'Constitutional and Fundamental Rights Aspects of Age Discrimination' in A. Numhauser-Henning and M. Rönnmar (eds), *Age Discrimination and Labour Law: Comparative and Conceptual Perspectives in the EU and Beyond* (Kluwer, The Netherlands, 2015).

117 1997 Treaty of Amsterdam.

In addition, age is included in the protection for equality found in the Article 21 of the EU Charter of Fundamental Rights,[118] and following the introduction of age equality in the Framework Directive, equality on grounds of age was recognised as a general principle of EU law in the case of *Mangold*.[119]

The protection against age discrimination is contained in Directive 2000/78. It applies to age in general, rather than being restricted to those of any particular age. Anyone of any age can make a claim in comparison with a person of a different age, and the protection is not directed only to the needs of older or younger workers. Recital 11 sets out the aims of age equality, and notes that age equality, as well as aiding the attainment of a high level of employment, social protection and quality of life, can also aid economic and social cohesion, and solidarity.[120] While age equality shares these features with other equality grounds, the Directive also recognizes that age discrimination is different, with special recitals applying to age only: age discrimination can be justified by legitimate employment policy,[121] and retirement ages can be retained.[122]

The Directive prohibits both direct and indirect discrimination on grounds of age.[123] In common with other grounds, indirect discrimination can be justified where there is a legitimate aim for any provision criterion or practice based on age, and the means of achieving that aim are appropriate and necessary. Also in common with other grounds, direct discrimination can be justified where, by reason of the nature of the particular occupational activities concerned or of the context in which they are carried out, age constitutes a genuine and determining occupational requirement, provided that the objective is legitimate and the requirement is proportionate.[124]

In contrast to the protection on other grounds, additional exceptions apply with respect to age equality, allowing direct discrimination to be justified. Article 6 provides:

> Member States may provide that differences of treatment on grounds of age shall not constitute discrimination, if, within the context of national law, they are objectively and reasonably justified by a legitimate aim, including legitimate employment policy, labour market and vocational

118 Incorporated into EU law in the Lisbon Treaty.

119 *Werner Mangold v Helm* ECJ 22 November 2005, C-144/04.

120 See recital 11 Directive 2000/78.

121 Recital 25 Directive 2000/78.

122 Recital 14 Directive 2000/78.

123 Article 2.

124 Article 4.

training objectives, and if the means of achieving that aim are appropriate and necessary.

Such differences of treatment may include, among others:

(a) the setting of special conditions on access to employment and vocational training, employment and occupation, including dismissal and remuneration conditions, for young people, older workers and persons with caring responsibilities in order to promote their vocational integration or ensure their protection;
(b) the fixing of minimum conditions of age, professional experience or seniority in service for access to employment or to certain advantages linked to employment;
(c) the fixing of a maximum age for recruitment which is based on the training requirements of the post in question or the need for a reasonable period of employment before retirement.

Thus, the EU framework for the protection against age discrimination reflects the multi-dimensional nature of age equality. In effect, the contradictions inherent in age equality, discussed in Part 1 above, are reflected in the strong commitment to age equality found in EU law, alongside recognition that age discrimination, including direct discrimination, can be justified. In particular, the economic dimension of age equality is reflected in the acceptance in the Directive of labour market needs and employment policy as potential justifications for age discrimination. However, it should be noted that direct age discrimination can only be justified for 'social policy objectives, such as those related to employment policy, the labour market or vocational training.... those legitimate aims are distinguishable from purely individual reasons particular to the employer's situation, such as cost reduction or improving competitiveness.'[125]

Whilst accepting employment policy related aims as potentially legitimate, the CJEU has recognised that such aims can be easy to assert and difficult to prove. In one of its early cases, the Court pointed out the need for caution in this regard, as 'mere generalisations concerning the capacity of a specific measure to contribute to employment policy, labour market or vocational training objectives are not enough to show that the aim of that measure is capable of justifying derogation from that principle and do not constitute evidence on the basis of which it could reasonably be considered that the means chosen are

125 *Age Concern England*, [2009 EUECJ C388/07] paragraph 46.

suitable for achieving that aim'.[126] In effect, then, an assertion that a measure serves a legitimate aim, as listed in the Directive, is insufficient of itself to justify less favourable treatment on the basis of age.

The extent to which the CJEU has had regard to the interplay of different aspects of age equality will be explored below with reference first to younger people.

Discrimination against Younger People

Discrimination against younger people can be both social and structural: stereotypical attitudes of employers can result in disadvantage, and labour market structures such as seniority based pay schemes can also result in disadvantage. Where age discrimination is the result of stereotypical and negative assumptions about being of a younger age, it can be challenged as directly discriminatory, and would not be justifiable under the provisions of the Directive. However, where discrimination is more structural, Article 6 of Directive 2000/78 provides explicit justification for some types of adverse treatment of younger workers, such as different remuneration conditions for young people to promote their vocational integration or ensure their protection, and the fixing of minimum conditions of age, professional experience or seniority in service for access to employment or to certain advantages linked to employment.

Although differential treatment of younger workers is provided for by the Directive, the CJEU sets reasonably high standards of justification for any such discriminatory practices. For example, in *Kücükdeveci*[127] a notice period was used for dismissal calculated on the basis of length of service, but ignoring employment before the age of 25. The CJEU rejected the employer's arguments and found the notice periods discriminatory. The reasons put forward by the employer were that it allowed flexibility to employers with respect to younger workers, given that these workers would find it easier to be mobile in terms of finding new work. The fact that this structural rule was based on a stereotype regarding the mobility of younger people meant that it could not be justified.

A common scenario in which younger workers can be subject to age discrimination is where age is used to set pay scales. Here the court has taken a varied approach, depending on whether the pay scale relies directly on age, and whether the reasons for the differential result according to age can be justified for other reasons. For example, in *Hennigs*[128] the court did not allow the setting of basic pay by reference to an employee's age. However, where pay

---

126 *Age Concern England*, [2009] EUECJ C388/07 paragraph 51.

127 *Kücükdeveci -v- Swedex GmbH & Co. KG* [2010] EUECJ C555/07.

128 *Hennigs v Eisenbahn-Bundesamt and Land Berlin v Mai* [2011] EUECJ C-298/10.

increments are awarded according to length of service, they can be lawful. For example, where differential pay rates are designed to reward loyalty and experience, they can be justified. However, providing higher pay at a particular age on the basis that older employees have additional financial needs was not justified: there was no evidence that young employees would not have family commitments, and older workers could have few such commitments.[129] In effect, to the extent that the different pay rates relied on stereotypes regarding financial needs at different ages, it could not be justified, but where length of service has a link to experience or other labour market reasons, it can be reasonably easily justified.[130] For example, in *Odar v Baxter Deutschland GmbH*[131] the CJEU accepted that the calculation of redundancy payments with reference to age could be justified. In this case, redundancy payments reduced as workers got closer to pension age, and the CJEU accepted that this was justified by the legitimate aim of protecting younger workers and helping their integration into employment.

Before an incremental pay scheme can be justified, it is also necessary to establish a link between the pay scheme and the aim pursued. In *Hütter v Technische Universität Graz*[132] the Court considered an age based pay scheme which discounted any time spent working or training before the age of 18. The aim for the exclusion of experience gained at a younger age was to ensure that there was no disadvantage for those who stayed in education for longer (thereby losing the chance to build up years of service); and to promote young people's entry into the labour market. The CJEU accepted that these aims were potentially justifiable but held that, because better ways to integrate young people could be identified, the scheme was not an appropriate means of achieving the aims.

In similar vein, the CJEU accepted as potentially legitimate a number of aims for an age discriminatory rule in *Abercrombie & Fitch Italia Srl v Antonino Bordonaro.*[133] Here, Italian law allowed a flexible form of employment similar to zero hours contracts to be offered to workers under 25 and over 55. Bordonaro was employed on such a contract until he turned 35 at which time his employ-

129 *Hennigs v Eisenbahn-Bundesamt and Land Berlin v Mai* [2011] EUECJ C-298/10 at para 70.

130 See also *Tyrolean Airways Tiroler Luftfahrt Gesellschaft mbH v Betriebsrat Bord der Tyrolean Airways Tiroler Luftfahrt Gesellschaft mbH* [2012] EUECJ C-132/11, where service with the particular airline was rewarded by additional pay. This was found not to be age discriminatory.

131 [2012] EUECJ C-152/11.

132 Case C-88/08.

133 *Abercrombie & Fitch Italia Srl v Antonino Bordonaro* Case C143/16 23 March 2017.

ment was ended. He claimed that this was discriminatory on grounds of age. The CJEU held that the Italian government's aims for the rule were potentially legitimate: promoting flexibility in the job market, fostering access for young people to the labour market and providing first employment opportunities for young people. The CJEU then left it to the national court to decide whether these aims were appropriate and necessary in light of its more detailed knowledge of the domestic legal landscape. In leaving much to the national court's discretion the CJEU did point out that while increased flexibility in the labour market may be a legitimate aim, it can be difficult to see why the burden of realising flexibility should be borne only by particular age groups; equally, it pointed out the need for a logical relationship of suitability and coherence between the aims and the means chosen to achieve those aims. Here, it questioned whether giving access to the labour market for one group (those under 25) whilst denying it to another (25–55 year olds) really could enhance recruitment, or whether instead it merely shifted the problem of unemployment onto another group of workers. While the Court made clear that the discrimination might be difficult to justify, and that aims and the means by which they are achieved need to correlate, the Court stopped short of determining whether the age based rules were justified on their facts, leaving this crucial question to the national courts.

A second issue that has arisen in relation to the age implications of pay schemes has been that of protecting employees' acquired rights. This raises age equality issues, as those who have acquired rights are likely to be older than those who have not. Sometimes changes to terms and conditions reduce their quality, but at other times changes are introduced to remove discriminatory terms, such as age related benefits. Where employers wish to amend terms and conditions of employment they can end up eroding employees' acquired rights or treating younger workers less favourably. This scenario was addressed in *Specht and ors v Land Berlin*,[134] in which a salary scheme was changed so that experience was used, instead of age, in setting pay. Existing staff were kept on the old age-based salary system, so as to preserve their acquired rights. This was challenged on the basis that the new system was age discriminatory because it perpetuated the old discriminatory system. The CJEU held that although the old age-based salary system was discriminatory, and its continuance in the new scheme was therefore also potentially discriminatory, the new system was justified. The new system was introduced with the aim of protecting the acquired rights of existing staff and had been accepted by the trade

134 C-501/12–C-541/12. The issues was also considered in *Hennigs and Mai*, EU:C:2011:560.

unions: its aims were legitimate and the means of achieving them were appropriate and necessary.

In sum, although age discrimination against younger workers is outlawed by the Directive on equal terms with age discrimination against older workers, structural discrimination does seem to be reasonably readily justified. Article 6(1) itself sets out explicitly examples of discriminatory practice that can be accepted, including setting of special conditions on access to employment and vocational training, separate remuneration and actions to promote integration in the workplace. This allows employers to continue with many age discriminatory practices such as setting pay with regard to experience, and awarding lower redundancy payments to younger workers. However, the CJEU has required employers to show a link between the legitimate aim pursued by a pay scheme and the means employed to achieve it, requiring that the means be necessary and appropriate. The Court has also been careful to ensure that stereotypical assumptions and prejudicial attitudes cannot be used to justify discrimination against younger workers.

Discrimination against Older Workers in General

As with discrimination against younger workers, the Directive prohibits reliance by employers on stereotypical or prejudicial assumptions about older workers. In addition, some specific types of workplace practice may disadvantage older workers, such as requirements that individuals be below a particular age to participate in training, and these too will need to be justified. This is specifically covered by Article 6 (1)(c) which states that fixing a maximum age for recruitment based on the training requirements or the need for a reasonable period of employment before retirement can be justified.

As with discrimination on other grounds, any claims for justification do need to be applicable on the facts, and the CJEU has paid fairly close regard to claims involving maximum recruitment ages for the purposes of training. In *Wolf v Stadt Frankfurt am Main*[135] the fire service imposed a maximum age of 30 for the recruitment of fire fighters on the basis that this was necessary to guarantee its operational capacity and proper functioning. Evidence was produced showing a diminution with age in respiratory capacity, musculature and endurance, particularly over the age of 45, and by 50 fire fighters no longer have the capacity for rescuing people. Although those over 45 could continue to work for the service on less onerous duties, it was felt necessary to require staff to start their career younger so as to give the fire service the benefit of a substantial period of service at full physical capacity, before being moved

135 Case C-229/08.

to other roles, and so to ensure full operational capacity for the fire service. Given the objective data on which the employer's position was based, the CJEU upheld the age-related rule. The aims were legitimate as linked to operational capacity, and the imposition of an age limit did not go beyond what was necessary to achieve that objective.

The need for a clear assessment of the facts before an age based policy on recruitment will be justified is confirmed in two later cases involving age limits on recruitment in the police. In *Mario Vital Pérez v Ayuntamiento de Oviedo*[136] recruitment to the police officers was limited to those under 30. The CJEU accepted that the rule served a legitimate aim of meeting training requirements and the need for a reasonable period of employment before retirement or transfer, however, a lack of evidence that these aims were met by the otherwise discriminatory rule meant that the rule was not upheld. In contrast, in *Gorka Salaberria Sorondo v Academia Vasca de Policia y Emergencias*, a maximum age of 35 for recruitment into the Basque Police and Emergency Services Academy was justified. The police academy had evidence of a decline in operational capacity after the age of 40, necessitating an earlier career start. Moreover, the nature of the role involved more physical roles with a higher degree of operational activity which could imply recourse to physical force.[137] In this respect, it could be contrasted with *Vital Pérez* where the local policing role was not so physical and included directing traffic and performing administrative tasks. These cases show that a clear evidence base is necessary if discrimination in recruitment is to be justified.

A further type of discrimination experienced by older workers relates to reduced access to benefits due to the proximity to retirement. *Toftgaard*[138] concerned a Danish law which allows for the award of three years 'availability pay' to civil servants in case of redundancy, in order to retain a pool of available staff in case of an increased demand. The aim of 'availability pay' is to enable the restructuring of the public administration by maintaining the availability of civil servants whilst at the same time protecting civil servants from undue personal and political pressure. However 'availability pay' is not paid to those over pensionable age, who are less likely to be under such pressure as they have alternative means of financial support, and equally are unlikely to be looking for alternative work if it were to become available. The CJEU upheld the claim that the rules are discriminatory on the basis of age. The rules did have a

136 *Mario Vital Pérez v Ayuntamiento de Oviedo* C-416/13.

137 *Gorka Salaberria Sorondo v Academia Vasca de Policia y Emergencias*, Case C-258/15.

138 *Dansk Jurist- og Økonomforbund, acting on behalf of Erik Toftgaard v. Indenrigs- og Sundhedsministeriet* Case number C-546/11.

legitimate aim but the means used to achieve the aim were not necessary, as the same objective could be achieved in a less discriminatory way. For example, staff of pensionable age could have been given a choice to either take pension, or to temporarily sacrifice pension and elect instead to take availability pay and make themselves available to work.

The Case of Retirement

The use of a state retirement age, although clearly based on age, is not of itself prohibited by Directive 2000/78, which applies without prejudice to national provisions laying down retirement ages.[139] However, despite the exclusion of state retirement ages from the coverage of the Directive, retirement cases have featured heavily in the CJEU case law. This is because the Directive still applies to the termination of employment once retirement ages are reached.[140] Thus, if employers rely on state retirement ages to terminate employment, this will amount to direct discrimination. In effect, then, mandatory retirement provisions applied by employers will still require justification under Article 6 of the Directive.[141]

Retirement is not mentioned in the justifications for different treatment listed in Article 6. However, the list is not exhaustive and in any event contains some broad categories, such as 'legitimate employment policy, labour market and vocational training objectives'. For example, using these objectives, the CJEU accepted that a default retirement age of 65 can be justified in order to enable employers to manage workforce planning, and allowed member states a level of discretion in defining legitimate employment or social policy aims even where not included in the Article 6(1) list.[142] As long as the aims relate to social policy with a public interest nature, rather than 'individual reasons particular to the employer's situation, such as cost reduction or improving competitiveness', they could be potentially legitimate aims. Moreover, the Court has allowed for a certain degree of flexibility for employers in pursuing these

---

139 Recital 14.

140 "... recital 14 ... does not in any way preclude the application of that directive to national measures governing the conditions for termination of employment contracts where the retirement age, thus established, has been reached." *Felix Palacios de la Villa v Cortefiel Servicios SA* (Case C-411/05) para 44.

141 This was confirmed in *R(on the application of The Incorporated Trustees of the National Council for Ageing (Age Concern England)) v Secretary of State for Business, Enterprise and Regulatory Reform*. C-388/07 Judgment of the Court (Third Chamber) of 5 March 2009.

142 *R(on the application of The Incorporated Trustees of the National Council for Ageing (Age Concern England)) v Secretary of State for Business, Enterprise and Regulatory Reform*. C-388/07 Judgment of the Court (Third Chamber) of 5 March 2009.

aims,[143] suggesting a fairly low level of scrutiny will be given by the Court in retirement cases. Indeed, the brief review of some of the CJEU cases which follows, reveals that while the Court has continued to review retirement provisions, requiring that they be justified, it has not challenged many mandatory retirement schemes.

Felix Palacios de la Villa v Cortefiel Servicios SA[144] was the first retirement case heard by the CJEU. Mr Palacios de la Villa challenged his retirement under an agreement which provided for a retirement age of 65, subject to the condition that retirement would only be enforced if workers had made sufficient contributions to be able to retire on a full pension. The CJEU confirmed that retirement was covered by the Directive and that high standards of justification would be required. However it then found that the mandatory retirement provision was justified as its aim was legitimate: promoting better access to employment by means of better distribution of work among different generations. Thus the CJEU readily accepted not only that the aim of redistributing work among different generations is legitimate, but also that retirement is an appropriate and necessary way to achieve this aim. This has been confirmed in much of the CJEU case law,[145] and reflects a clear recognition by the Court of the economic and structural dimensions of age equality, based on the demographic aspects of age discrimination, as discussed above.

However, despite the fairly ready acceptance of retirement in the case, the Court has imposed a level of scrutiny of the justification for age discrimination, requiring that claims made by the employer be justified on their facts. For example, in *Palacios* the Court gave weight to the fact that the retirement provisions were contained in a collective agreement and only applied where full pension had accrued. The fact that Mr Palacios had accrued a full pension was therefore a relevant factor in determining the proportionality of the retirement provision.

Although, following *Palacios*, it could be that mandatory retirement would be hard to justify in the absence of collective agreements and adequate pension provision, later retirement cases have not taken such an approach, and have instead allowed for mandatory retirement to be justified even where the individual concerned had little pension provision. Thus in the very similar case

143 At para 46.

144 Case C-411/05.

145 *Petersen v Berufungsausschuss fur Zahn fur den BezirkWestfalen-Lippe* Judgment of the CJEU of 12 January 2010, Case- C-341/08; *Rosenbladt v OellerkingGebaudereinigungsges. mbH* Judgment of the CJEU 12 October 2010, Case C-45/09. *Hörnfeldt v Meddelande* Case C-141/11 Judgment of the CJEU 5 July 2012.

of *Rosenbladt*,[146] mandatory retirement was allowed, even though the pension provision available was much lower as Ms Rosenbladt's hours were much lower: the CJEU still accepted that retirement was objectively justified, as its aim was the better distribution of work between the generations, and in the context that retirement was only imposed where there was eligibility for a pension. The Court upheld the necessity and appropriateness of the agreement despite the fact that when applied to Ms Rosenbladt personally, her pension provision was insufficient for her needs. The Court recognized the limitations of the justifications on the facts, but equally recognized that member states require some discretion in the area of social policy.

Again the Court has continued to give weight to the labour market and economic policy dimensions to age equality in its reasoning, rather than focusing on its impact on the individual. The employment policy aim of balancing the interests of older workers against those of younger workers is usually based on assumptions that the older workers will already have accrued pension and so can afford to hand over the job to younger workers whose financial need is greater. Given that this was not the case in Ms Rosenbladt's case, the Court could have considered whether it was proportionate to implement the retirement provision in her individual case, but instead it upheld the general provision regarding mandatory retirement. Similarly, in *Hörnfeldt v Meddelande*[147] a part time worker challenged a rule requiring retirement at 67, but the CJEU upheld the blanket rule on retirement: although compulsory retirement resulted in some hardship to the individual because of his individual pension level, it was still proportionate.

The reluctance of the Court to address the individual hardship that generalised retirement rules can cause is perhaps unsurprising considering how complex such an assessment could become given the range of individual choices that could give rise to lower income in older age,[148] but nonetheless it would seem to confirm that the Court has not addressed some of the social and intersectional dimensions to age discrimination.

Yet, despite this tendency to maintain existing labour market structures, the Court has set higher standards when tackling the use of stereotypes by employers in implementing retirement schemes. Thus, where legitimate aims for retirement have a discriminatory basis, they have not always been found to be justified. In particular, the Court has been reluctant to accept that retirement is justified on the basis that performance declines with age. For example, in

146 *Rosenbladt -v- Ollerking Gebaudereinigungsges.mbH* C-45/09.

147 Case C-141/11 Judgment of the CJEU 5 July 2012.

148 Refer to page 22 above.

Petersen v Berufungsausschuss fur Zahn fur den Bezirk Westfalen-Lippe[149] a retirement age of 68 for dentists working in public health care was challenged. The government tried to justify the rule on the basis that that 'general experience' indicated that after the age of 68 dentists' work performance was likely to decline; and that it was necessary to free up jobs and career opportunities for young dentists. This second aim was accepted by the CJEU, but the first was not: the assumption that performance deteriorates after the age of 68 was based on stereotypes, and indeed there was evidence that the requirement to retire at 68 did not apply to dentists operating in the private sector. Thus the claim that there was a risk to public health from older dentists was not borne out by the evidence.

Similarly, in *Prigge v Deutsche Lufthansa AG*[150] the Court rejected the use of stereotypical assumptions about deterioration of performance as justification for mandatory retirement of pilots at the age of 60, in accordance with a collective agreement with the aim of maintaining safety. This case was considered under the genuine occupational requirement exception contained in Article 4(1), which also requires that exceptions be justified as proportionate means of achieving a legitimate aim. The Court found that retirement was not proportionate because international and national rules, as well as the practice of other airlines, did not require retirement at the age of 60. Again stereotyped assumptions regarding age and deteriorating performance were not allowed to justify retirement. These cases can be contrasted with *Wolf*[151] and *Gorka Salaberria Sorondo*,[152] above, where the reduction in capacity with age was accepted as justification for maximum ages for training, where there was detailed scientific data used to substantiate the claims. It could therefore be that Court might accept retirement as an option if backed by reliable data justifying retirement at a particular age, but it will not accept generalised assumptions based on stereotype.

The CJEU has also been faced with other cases involving somewhat indirect stereotypes or prejudicial assumptions by employers and it has not always taken a consistent approach on this matter. The first more indirectly stereotyped assumption that the Court has faced involves the aim of ensuring a mix of ages in the workforce. For example, *Georgiev v Technicheski universitet—Sofia, filial Plovdiv*[153] involved retirement rules for academic staff in

149 Case C-341/08.
150 Case C447/09.
151 Case C-229/08.
152 Case C-258/15.
153 C-250/09 and C-268/09.

Higher Education. The rules in question required that staff at 65 move from permanent contracts to one year contracts, for a maximum of 3 years. In effect, mandatory retirement was imposed at 68. The Court accepted that the rules could be justified for the legitimate aim of encouraging recruitment and retention of younger academics, but it also appeared to accept as legitimate the aim of ensuring 'the quality of teaching and research by renewing the teaching staff through the employment of younger professors'.[154] It also confirmed the importance of maintaining a mix of different generations in order 'to promote an exchange of experiences and innovation, and thereby the development of quality of teaching and research at universities.'[155] These latter aims seem to accept stereotypical thinking that the quality of teaching will be maintained by replacing older professors with younger ones. The need for a balance of ages was accepted again in *Fuchs and Kohler v Land Hessen*,[156] in which the court accepted, among others, that the aim of establishing a balanced age structure was a legitimate aim for the mandatory retirement scheme. It is not always particularly clear why an age mix is needed. One reason could be to ensure good handover of skills, to avoid large groups of workers reaching pension age at the same time and opting for retirement, potentially leading to a skills shortage. Such reasoning may not involve veiled stereotypes. However, age mix can also be based on prejudicial and stereotyped assumptions about reduced skills and adaptability of older workers. It may also veil prejudicial preferences by students or customers to be served or taught by younger staff.

A final aim for retirement ages that has been accepted by courts can also be understood to be an indirect form of stereotyped assumptions about a decline in performance as workers age, albeit disguised as a concern for their dignity.[157] This is the aim of avoiding capability disputes at the end of working life. For example in *Rosenbladt*[158] the CJEU accepted the aim of avoiding the dismissal of employees 'on the ground that they are no longer capable of working, which may be humiliating for those who have reached an advanced age.' In *Fuchs* the Court accepted as legitimate the aim of preventing 'possible disputes

154 At para 42.

155 In examining whether the measures in question were 'appropriate and necessary', the Court also took account of the fact that those affected had pension entitlements, and that a mandatory retirement age of 68 was five years higher than the statutory age in Bulgaria. Thus professors were already 'allowed to pursue their career for a relatively long period' (paragraph 54).

156 C-159/10 and C-160/10.

157 See page 17 ff where this issue is addressed.

158 At para 43.

concerning employees' fitness to work beyond a certain age'[159] In *Hörnfeldt v Meddelande*[160] the CJEU confirmed as legitimate the aim of avoiding 'a situation in which employment contracts are terminated in situations which are humiliating for elderly workers'.[161] This aim is based not only on an assumption that performance deteriorates with age, but also that older workers are not likely to recognize this.

The early case law of the CJEU asserted that although the Directive operated without prejudice to state retirement, it nonetheless applied to the use of retirement by employers, such that the implementation of retirement schemes would need to be justified as a proportionate means to achieve a legitimate aim. However, as the case law shows, the potential created by the Directive to challenge the use of retirement has not been fully realized. The Court has been fairly ready to accept that retirement is justified by aims such as intergenerational solidarity and the freeing-up of jobs for younger workers being accepted as legitimate. Moreover, Court has been somewhat inconsistent in its treatment of aims which rely on assumptions regarding a decline in performance with age; some of these have been rejected, such as *Petersen*, whilst elsewhere they have been accepted in the name of avoiding the risk of undignified capability proceedings late in career.[162]

Conclusion on EU Law on Age

The less than robust approach to tackling the age inequality that is inherent in retirement reflects the ambiguity in the approach of the CJEU to age discrimination more generally. The Court has taken a fairly generous approach to identifying legitimate aims for potential age discrimination in cases involving young workers as well as older workers and retirees. This perhaps reflects the complexity that can be seen in the case for age inequality as discussed above, whereby the interaction of social with economic and structural dimensions to age equality was seen to be complicated and at times contradictory.

Whilst the CJEU has accepted a range of aims for age discrimination as legitimate, it has been more rigorous in requiring reliance on those aims to be necessary and backed by evidence. For example, although maximum ages for recruitment can serve a legitimate aim of ensuring a period working on full

---

159 *Fuchs* at para 50.

160 Case C-141/11 Judgment of the CJEU 5 July 2012.

161 At para 34.

162 For further discussion see E. Dewhurst, 'Proportionality Assessments of Mandatory Retirement Measures: Uncovering Guidance for National Courts in Age Discrimination Cases' (2016) 45(1) *Industrial Law Journal* 60.

duties, the Court has only accepted such requirements once the employer has shown evidence of a decline, rather than relying on generalized assumptions.

In effect, the CJEU has addressed stereotype and the reliance on prejudice, while leaving intact some of the more structural and institutionalised aspects of age, which are embedded within the labour market.[163] Thus changes to retirement, and differential terms of employment for younger or older workers have been relatively easy to justify, with significant discretion left to member states in implementing the Directive. In contrast, where rules seem to be based on stereotypes (e.g. that capacity will decline with age, or that younger workers will not have dependants) the CJEU has been more willing to intervene. The CJEU appears to address some of the social dimensions of age equality through tackling stereotypes, but the more structural aspects of age discrimination (retirement, age based payment systems) remain.

Whilst this can be explained as a response to the sometimes contradictory dimensions of age equality, the failure to fully address the social aims of age equality leaves particular groups more vulnerable than others. For example, the CJEU failed to address intersectional issues in *Rosenbladt*, which involved a female part timer cleaner, on low pay and in a stereotypically female form of work. Instead, the Court's response to her financial difficulty was the rather unsympathetic observation that the provisions mandating retirement did not prevent her from seeking another job.[164] The failure of the CJEU to address individual disadvantage, but rather to uphold current labour market structures suggests that the social dimension of equality loses out to the economic in the context of the EU law.

UK

The UK response to age discrimination was at first non-statutory, with measures such as the Code of Practice on Age Diversity in Employment, which aimed to raise awareness about age discrimination, highlight the benefits of employing an age diverse workforce and reverse early retirement trends. These soft law measures were ineffective in themselves to address the multi-dimensional

163 See M. Freedland and L. Vickers, 'Age Discrimination and EU labour rights law' in A. Bogg, C. Costello and A. Davies (eds), *A Research Handbook on EU Labour* Law (Cheltenham, Edward Elgar, 2016).

164 See M. Freedland and L. Vickers, 'Age Discrimination and EU labour rights law' in A. Bogg, C. Costello and A. Davies (eds), *A Research Handbook on EU Labour* Law (Cheltenham, Edward Elgar, 2016).

problem of age discrimination,[165] and in 2006, the UK implemented its own legislation in response to the EU Equality Directive 2000/78. The Employment Equality (Age) Regulations 2006 prohibited direct and indirect discrimination on the grounds of age, as well as harassment and victimization. It largely followed the Directive in allowing for direct discrimination to be justified where it is a proportionate means of achieving a legitimate aim. The Regulations were replaced by the Equality Act 2010, but continue to mirror the Equality Directive by prohibiting discrimination except where it can be justified as a proportionate means of achieving a legitimate aim. While the UK courts interpret the Equality Act in accordance with the parent Directive, the Employment Appeal Tribunal has held that the level of scrutiny with which proportionality is reviewed is higher in UK domestic law than under the Directive, with particular reference to the need to consider whether there are other, less discriminatory, measures which would have achieved the legitimate aim.[166]

The 2006 Regulations provided for a default retirement age of 65, although this particular approach to retirement was short-lived, as discussed below, and mandatory retirement was abolished in 2011. The 2006 Regulations were replaced by the Equality Act 2010, which includes age as a protected characteristic and so provides protection against age discrimination as part of its framework of protection against discrimination on a range of grounds.

As well as prohibiting age discrimination, the Equality Act also allows employers to provide additional benefits, facilities or services such as additional pay or holiday entitlement to accrue with each year of service, up to a period of five years. If benefits are accrue over a longer time period they will only be lawful if the employer can justify them on the basis of business need.[167]

Although the Equality Act covers all age groups, most of the case law has involved discrimination against older workers, and very few have involved harassment or victimization.

---

165 See A. Blackham, *Extending Working Life for Older Workers: Age Discrimination Law, Policy and Practice* (Hart Publishing, Oxford, 2016). For an evaluation of the impact of the code of practice, see D. Jones Evaluation of the Code of Practice on Age Diversity in Employment, Research Brief RBX 6/00 (Nottingham: Department for Education and Employment June 2000).

166 *R Sargeant & Ors v London Fire and Emergeny Planning Authority and Ors* (2018) UKEAT/0137/17/LA.

167 Equality Act 2010 Schedule 9 Part 2, para 10.

Discrimination against Younger Workers

Outside the non-discrimination framework, the labour market in the UK continues to use age in relation to many of its structures. For example, the National Minimum Wage Act provides for lower rates of pay for younger people under 25; and reduced levels statutory redundancy payments continue to be payable for younger employees, with half a week's pay for employment under the age of 22, one week's pay for employment between 22 and 41, and one and half week's pay for employment over the age of 41.[168]

UK cases of discrimination against younger workers echo the cases that have arisen elsewhere in the EU, and have involved both reliance on stereotypes, such as assumptions of incompetence in younger workers,[169] and less favourable terms and conditions governing redundancy or pay that those available to older workers.

Both direct and indirect discrimination can be justified where proportionate, and most of the cases involving discrimination against younger workers have not focussed so much on the difference between the two types of discrimination, but rather on when and how age discrimination can be justified.

In *Lockwood v Department of Work and Pensions*[170] the claimant was paid a lower redundancy payment than her older colleagues. Lockwood took voluntary redundancy at the age of 26, and was paid around half the amount of compensation than she would have been had she been aged over 35, due to age related severance terms. Although the Court of Appeal viewed this as directly discriminatory on grounds of age, it held that it could be justified as a proportionate means of achieving a legitimate aim. The additional redundancy pay awarded to older workers aimed to create a 'proportionate financial cushion until alternative employment is found or as a bridge into retirement',[171] and recognized both that the older workers were more likely to have family responsibilities, and that they might also find it more difficult to find alternative work. The Court of Appeal accepted that the use of age to act as indicative of financial need was not accurate in Lockwood's case, but took the view that it was not disproportionate for the original Employment Tribunal to conclude that the resulting age discrimination was justified, and that it would not be practicable

168 Employment Rights Act 1996 section 162(2).

169 See for example, the ET decisions in *Osborne and another v Gondhia and others t/a Rutaba Partnership*, ET/3401426/2014 & ET/3401427/2014 and *Roberts v (1) Cash Zone (Camberley Ltd); (2) Cullen*, ET/2701804/2012.

170 [2013] EWCA Civ 1195.

171 Ibid. at para 15.

to assess severance payments on an individualized basis.[172] A similar approach can be seen in *MacCulloch v Imperial Chemical Industries plc*[173] where the use of age as a multiplier for the calculation of redundancy payments was accepted as legitimate on the basis that it encouraged older workers to leave, thereby creating jobs for younger workers, and that it reflected the fact that older workers can find it harder to find new work.

Although in *MacCulloch* the EAT held that the original tribunal had not properly assessed the proportionality of the scheme, the case, read with *Lockwood*, illustrates some of the tensions that can arise between achieving fairness at an individual level and creating administratively workable systems. In addition, the fairly ready acceptance of the use of age as proxy for financial need demonstrates the relative ease with which age discrimination can be justified in the UK,[174] despite the claim in *Sargeant* that a higher level of scrutiny of proportionality is applied.[175]

Discrimination against Older Workers

As with discrimination against younger workers, many of the discrimination cases involving older workers have involved age related stereotypes, such as assumptions about receptivity to training, and reduced physical or mental capacity. Other cases have resulted from the fact that labour market structures are infused with age; for example, employers have discriminated against older employees in an attempt to prevent them enjoying age or service related benefits such as increased redundancy payments; and older staff have challenged age based rules such as maximum ages for training.

Age Related Stereotypes

Where employers treat older workers less favourably due to stereotyped assumptions, the treatment amounts to direct discrimination. One stereotypical and ageist assumption relates to the receptiveness of older workers to change. For example, in *Dixon v Croglin Estate Co Ltd*[176] an Employment Tribunal found that age was a material factor in a decision to dismiss a 58 year old game keeper

172 See the discussion in 'Disadvantage' above on the difficulty of assuming that disadvantage correlates with age in any given case.

173 (EAT) 0119/08/RN.

174 A. Blackham, 'Falling on Their Feet: Young Workers, Employment and Age Discrimination' (2015) 44(2) *Industrial Law Journal* 246.

175 *R Sargeant & Ors v London Fire and Emergeny Planning Authority and Ors* (2018) UKEAT/0137/17/LA.

176 (2011) ET No 2502955/2011.

on capability grounds. Dixon, Head Keeper for an estate, was seen as being responsible when the estate's grouse shooting earnings started to fall, because in the employer's view, he was 'set in his ways', and 'unlikely to change'. The employer also suggested that he would not be able to do 'all the GPS computer work'. The employer offered no justification for these comments, and the Employment Tribunal held that Dixon's treatment was directly discriminatory. Similarly in the case of *James v Gina Shoes*[177] a 58 year old salesman was dismissed as his employer made it clear that they felt that Mr James' age had 'caused him not to meet their expectations'. During a grievance meeting the employer made comments such as 'you can't teach an old dog new tricks'. Again, this treatment was found to be directly discriminatory. A further example of ageist stereotypes can be seen in *Gomes v Henworth Limited t/a Winkworth Estate Agents*,[178] where the judgement that a 59 year old estate agent was 'better suited to a traditional estate agency' was found to have led to direct discrimination, because in the context in which it was used, the word 'traditional' was a reference to being old-fashioned and set in her ways: the word would not have been used of a younger employee.

The cases show that the UK courts are fairly robust in challenging any reliance by employers on stereotypes and prejudicial assumptions based on age. Courts have found actions reliant on such assumptions to amount to direct discrimination. Although direct discrimination can potentially be justified, reliance on such stereotypes would be very difficult for employers to justify.

Age Related Rules

A second example of discrimination against older workers can be seen in relation to age related rules. Some of these apply to training, where older age may lead to the denial of access to or funding for training. Others relate to changes to workplace structures which can have a detrimental effect on existing workers, resulting in indirect discrimination. As with direct discrimination, indirect discrimination is prima facie unlawful unless it can be justified as a proportionate means of achieving a legitimate aim.

For example, in *Homer v Chief Constable of West Yorkshire Police*[179] a new grading system was introduced which required a law degree in order to reach the top tier. The requirement was imposed on all staff, but it disadvantaged Mr Homer because he was due to retire and did not have sufficient time before retirement to make it worth his while undertaking the three years of training

177 [2011] UKEAT/0384/11/DM.

178 16 February 2017, case number 3323775/2016.

179 [2012] UKSC 15.

that would be required to achieve the highest salary tier. The Supreme Court held that the law degree requirement was indirectly discriminatory, and would need to be justified. When the case returned to the first tier Employment Tribunal the requirement was found not to be justified. It had a legitimate aim (of recruiting and retaining staff of an appropriate calibre) and the new grading system was an appropriate and necessary way of achieving the aim, but nonetheless, it was not necessary to impose it on all existing legal advisors.

Homer's case also illustrates the difficulty which can arise when changes are made to terms and conditions of employment, as these will necessarily have an age related impact. However, changes are allowed where they serve a legitimate aim and are proportionate, which will be the case in many instances, albeit not in Homer's; otherwise no changes to terms of employment could be allowed.

Age Related Expense

As discussed above, the labour market includes a number of age related rules such as enhanced redundancy provision, and these have been largely continued since the introduction of age discrimination laws. Where they have been challenged, they have been justified on the basis that they can provide a cushion for those who may have increased financial needs, or who may find it difficult to find new employment. However, whilst increased payments obviously benefit those to whom they are paid, the obligation to pay at a higher rate can also lead employers to try to avoid such payments, with resulting disadvantage to those who are eligible. Where employers have dismissed staff in order to avoid higher redundancy payments, the age discriminatory effect has been justified as a means to reduce the financial liabilities of the employer. This is despite the fact that costs alone are not allowed to justify discrimination. For example, in *Woodcock v Cumbria Primary Care Trust*[180] an employee, the Chief Executive of an NHS trust, was made redundant after a work reorganisation. His contract provided that if he was employed past his 50th birthday, he would be entitled to enhanced pension benefits that would cost his employer between £500k and £1m. The employer dismissed him a month before his 50th birthday, before conducting the appropriate consultation with him, in order to avoid paying the enhanced pension benefits. Mr Woodcock claimed that he had been directly discriminated against on the grounds of his age, and the Employment Tribunal agreed that the dismissal was timed to avoid Mr Woodcock reaching pensionable age. In terms of justification, the main justification was clearly to save the

180 [2012] EWCA Civ 330.

additional and considerable extra costs that were payable once Mr Woodcock reached 50.

In terms of justification, the usual rule in discrimination is that costs alone cannot be used to justify discrimination.[181] Here, the Court of Appeal held that the discrimination was not being justified on cost grounds alone: although the aim was to avoid Mr Woodcock being the beneficiary of a pure windfall by being in post at age 50, he was given notice for the additional reason that he was legitimately and genuinely being made redundant.

A second example of the use of costs to justify age discrimination can be seen in *HM Land Registry v Benson & Ors*[182] where it was accepted that an employer could base its selection criteria for redundancy primarily on cost. The employer wished to make as many voluntary redundancies as possible within a fixed budget. Workers aged 50–54 were entitled to extensive benefits under the Civil Service Compensation Scheme, making them much more expensive to make redundant. As a result, they were not chosen for redundancy. The employees claimed that it was discriminatory to rely on selection criteria based on the amount of compensation that would be paid, as it disadvantaged employees aged between 50 and 54 who wished to be made redundant. The employer's aim of reducing overall headcount was legitimate, and there was no alternative criterion for the employer to adopt in order to achieve this aim. Moreover, the court noted that impact of the discriminatory criterion was not as severe as in many discrimination cases since the claimants did not lose their jobs, or suffer other benefits other than the chance to take advantage of a 'windfall'.

As with the case of discrimination against younger workers, these examples demonstrate that the UK courts are reasonably willing to justify age discrimination in situations where discrimination is the result of age infused labour market structures, such as age-discriminatory pay or compensation structures cases. In contrast, a stronger line is taken where age stereotypes cause less favourable treatment.

The Case of Retirement

As discussed above, the issue of retirement is contentious in terms of age equality, with compulsory retirement both strongly embedded in workplace structures, while equally clearly amounting to *prima facie* age discrimination. The Age Regulations introduced in 2006 attempted to create a compromise by simultaneously encouraging employees to work beyond retirement whilst

181 *Cross v British Airways plc* [2005] IRLR 423.

182 *Her Majesty's Land Registry v Benson and others* UKEAT/0197/11/RN.

allowing employers to require them to leave. This was achieved by allowing compulsory retirement only when the employee had been given the option to request to continue to work past the age of 65.[183] At the same time, employers were only obliged to consider such requests, not to accept them. If employers decided to refuse a request to continue working, no reason needed to be given. The 'right to request' procedure thus created very mixed messages: the required notification of the right to request to continue to work before compulsory retirement could be lawful gave the impression that employees had a choice as to when to retire, yet in fact employers were under no obligation to grant requests.

In any event, the right to request procedure was short lived and abolished in 2011. The final result of the legislative changes was that under the Equality Act 2010, mandatory retirement amounts to direct discrimination and is only lawful if objectively justified as a proportionate means to achieve a legitimate aim.

Of course, in considering whether retirement can be justified in any particular case, courts will refer to the case law of the CJEU, discussed above. Two cases have also been heard in the higher courts in England, in which employers have sought to justify reliance on mandatory retirement.

In *Seldon v Clarkson Wright and Jakes*[184] the Supreme Court confirmed[185] that reading the Equality Act 2010 to comply with the Directive and the case law of the CJEU, the aims which can justify direct discrimination, such as retirement, will need to serve objectives of a public interest nature and be consistent with the social policy aims of the state. The means used must also be proportionate, that is both appropriate to the aim and reasonably necessary to achieve it.[186]

Mr Seldon, a partner in a law firm, claimed age discrimination when he was made to retire in accordance with the rules of the partnership agreement that had adopted a mandatory retirement age for partners at 65.[187] The firm sought to justify reliance on mandatory retirement on grounds that had been accepted

183 Or later if their contractual retirement age was later than 65. At the same time, the bar on claiming unfair dismissal and redundancy for those over the age of 65 was removed, thereby protecting those who chose to continue to work.

184 *Seldon v Clarkson Wright and Jakes* [2012] UKSC 16.

185 *Seldon* para 52.

186 *Seldon* para 55.

187 The case started under the Age Regulations (2006) when there was still a default retirement age, but it applied to the context of a partnership agreement rather than the employment relationship, and so the legal question turned on the question of whether the retirement could be objectively justified. It is thus of relevance to the legal context under the Equality Act 2010.

as legitimate by the CJEU, including enabling employers to manage workforce planning; promoting better access to employment for younger workers; and the aim of avoiding disputes relating to employees' ability to perform their duties beyond the age of 65. Applied in the context of the law firm, mandatory retirement at 65 enabled associate solicitors to be given the opportunity of partnership after a reasonable period by ensuring a reasonable turnover of staff (creating employment opportunities for younger staff);[188] it facilitated workforce planning by having a realistic expectation as to when vacancies would arise (workforce planning);[189] and it contributed to a congenial and supportive culture in the firm because it reduced the need to manage partners' performance at the end of careers (avoiding capability disputes).[190]

Thus the Supreme Court accepted that the use of mandatory retirement could be justified by relying on 'dignity' and 'intergenerational fairness' as legitimate aims. Although the Supreme Court endorsed the use of these aims as legitimate, it did note that it was only the legitimacy of the aim that was being decided: the parties still had to show that, on the facts, the reliance on the legitimate aim was necessary and proportionate. Lady Hale also noted that the 'assumptions underlying these objectives look suspiciously like stereotyping.'[191] Although accepting that the aims had been recognized in the CJEU case law, Lady Hale was clear that the aim of upholding the dignity of older workers by avoiding performance management should be applied very carefully in practice, ensuring that the aim must be justified on the particular circumstances of the case.

The acceptance of the dignity and intergenerational aims of retirement by the Supreme Court are not surprising given the guidance available from the CJEU. However the fact that both aims can be contested as reliant on either age based stereotypes regarding declining capacity with age (the dignity aim) or on contested economic assumptions about the labour market (intergenerational

---

188 *Felix Palacios de la Villa v Cortefiel Servicios SA* (Case C-411/05), *Petersen v Berufungsausschuss fur Zahn fur den Bezirk Westfalen-Lippe* Judgment of the CJEU of 12 January 2010, Case-C-341/08; *Rosenbladt v OellerkingGebaudereinigungsges.mbH* Judgment of the CJEU 12 October 2010, Case C-45/09, *Hörnfeldt v Meddelande* Case C-141/11 Judgment of the CJEU 5 July 2012.

189 *The Incorporated Trustees of the National Council on Aging v. Secretary of State for Business (The Age Concern case)* Case C-388/07.

190 *Rosenbladt v OellerkingGebaudereinigungsges.mbH* Judgment of the CJEU 12 October 2010, Case C-45/09, *Hörnfeldt v Meddelande* Case C-141/11 Judgment of the CJEU 5 July 2012.

191 *Seldon* at para 57.

justice aims) is of note.[192] The Court accepted that age discrimination was different from other grounds of discrimination because it is not 'binary in nature' but can be seen as a 'continuum which changes over time';[193] and that 'younger people will eventually benefit from a provision which favours older employees';[194] thus accepting the fair innings and complete life views of age equality. Yet, as discussed above, such thinking can be contested, as not all will have experienced their career 'innings' as fair; and it can also play into an agenda in which different generations are perceived as in conflict with each other, with older people taking an unfair share of social resource.[195]

Having accepted that the employer's aims were legitimate, the case was remitted to a new tribunal to determine whether the pursuit of these aims was proportionate on the facts. In *Seldon v Clarkson Wright & Jakes (No. 2)* the EAT ruled that the enforced retirement at 65 of the equity partner was justified. One further matter that arose in the case was whether the employer had to justify not only the use of age to determine retirement, but the use of the specific age of 65. On this issue, the EAT noted that if the particular age had to be justified, then it would be impossible to justify a retirement age at all: it would always be possible to add an extra year or month to the age and show that this age was less discriminatory.[196]

This approach seem reasonable, and is consistent with both Lady Hale's position in the Supreme Court that if retirement rules are generally justified, then their consequences are likely to be so too, and the case of *Hörnfeldt v Meddelande*[197] where the CJEU confirmed that a blanket rule on retirement could be justified, even if it resulted in some hardship to the individual. This approach can also be seen in the House of Lords' case of *Reynolds*[198] where Lord Hoffman pointed out that 'a line must be drawn somewhere. All that is necessary is that it should reflect a difference between the substantial majority of the people on either side of the line.'[199]

---

192 See further S. Manfredi and L. Vickers, "Age equality and Retirement: squaring the circle" (2013) 42 (1) *Industrial Law Journal* 61 and S. Manfredi and L. Vickers, 'Meeting the challenges of active ageing in the workplace: is the abolition of retirement the answer?' (2013) 4 (4) *European Labour Law Journal* 251.

193 *Seldon* at para 4.

194 Ibid.

195 See discussion at page 32 above.

196 Employment Appeal Tribunal [2014] IRLR 748, 13 May 2014.

197 Case C-141/11 Judgment of the CJEU 5 July 2012.

198 *R (Reynolds) v Secretary of Sate for Work and Pensions* [2005] UKHL 37. See also B. Hepple, Equality: the Legal Framework (2nd Ed) (Hart Publishing, Oxford, 2014) at p 80.

199 *Reynolds* at para 41.

In effect, UK courts have upheld general rules even if they create individual hardship, despite the fact that they take a rather different approach to individual cases in relation to other equality grounds.[200] However, the acceptance of generalised solutions to complex factual questions such as whether retirement is proportionate in a given case,[201] together with the fairly ready acceptance of contested dignity and intergenerational justice grounds for justifying discrimination, demonstrates the struggle courts have had in reconciling the competing demands of the economic, structural and social dimensions of age equality.[202]

A second UK case involving retirement is *Harrod v Chief Constable of West Midlands Police*,[203] in which police officers were compulsorily retired. The police force had needed to make reductions in staff numbers and the only lawful way to do so was by the application of a special police regulation[204] that allows for enforced retirement once an officer has served for 30 years, thereby qualifying for a pension of two thirds average pensionable pay. The police officers claimed that the use the regulation was indirectly discriminatory on grounds of age, as others with less service were not required to retire. The employer justified the use of the regulation because it was the only lawful means by which they could reduce their staff numbers, because of rules restricting the use of redundancy for police officers. The Court of Appeal found that the decision to compulsorily retire the police offers was justified as no other method of selection was lawful: the high degree of job security available to police officers left very little discretion to the employer and so the use of the regulation was proportionate. Again the embedded nature of age discriminatory rules in many workplace practices meant that the Court had to balance social and economic factors in considering the lawfulness of compulsory retirement.

Intersectional Claims Including Age

Under the Equality Act 2010, claims can only be brought on single grounds. Although the Equality Act as originally drafted allows for claims for combined discrimination on the basis of two characteristics, this has not been brought

200 *Cadman* v *Health & Safety Executive* [2006] IRLR 969.

201 Despite the fact that the concept of proportionality usually requires individual rather than 'one size fits all' solutions. See M Rubenstein, EOR 01/02/11 p 25.

202 E. Dewhurst, 'Proportionality Assessments of Mandatory Retirement Measures: Uncovering Guidance for National Courts in Age Discrimination Cases' (2016) 45(1) *Industrial Law Journal* 60.

203 [2017] EWCA Civ 191.

204 Regulation A19 of the Police Pensions Regulations 1987.

into force. Cases have been brought raising issues of age and sex discrimination together, however tribunals have only ruled on each single ground rather than viewing the characteristics together. For example, in *O'Reilly v BBC and others*[205] a 51 year old TV presenter, Miriam O'Reilly, was informed that she was no longer required, as the presenter line-up for the show she had presented was to be 'refreshed' in order to attract a larger audience share following its move to a prime time slot. The Employment Tribunal found that the BBC had been looking to replace presenters with younger people, to appeal to a younger audience. The tribunal did not allow the BBC to rely on the assumed prejudice of younger viewers to justify the age discrimination that had occurred. However, although the tribunal considered the issue of combined discrimination, it rejected the claim that gender had been a factor in the BBC's decision, either on its own, or in combination with age.

Conclusion on Age Discrimination in the UK

This review of the protection against age discrimination in the UK demonstrates its compliance with the EU age equality framework. Like the EU law from which it is derived, the UK too has been challenged to create a consistent and coherent response to the multi-dimensional aspects of age equality, discussed in Part 1 above. This is reflected in the fairly limited scrutiny applied in age cases, together with the acceptance of the continued use of age as a criterion in calculating redundancy pay, wages and work benefits. These cases also illustrate how age has continued to be embedded in labour market structures in the UK. The fairly relaxed acceptance of the justification of mandatory retirement in the cases that have come before the courts could also be taken to reflect a somewhat ambivalent approach of the courts to tackling structural aspects of age inequality. However, despite the fact that where challenged, mandatory retirement has been found to be justified, it should be borne in mind that the removal of default retirement ages, and the requirement for its use to be justified represents a significant change from the previous norm of retirement at the age of 65. This will have had a big impact in practice, an impact which does not show if the focus remains on cases that are litigated. Indeed, recent figures from the Department of Work and Pensions in the UK show that men and women are increasingly staying at work beyond the state pension age.[206]

---

205 London Central Employment Tribunal, case number 22004223/2010.

206 See DWP data available at https://www.gov.uk/government/uploads/system/uploads/attachment_data/file/642157/economic-labour-market-status-of-individuals-aged-50-and-over-since-1950.pdf (accessed 5 January 2018).

In terms of protection against age discrimination more generally, UK courts have taken steps to address some of the social dimensions of equality, with a more robust approach in discrimination cases which involve reliance on stereotype or prejudicial assumptions based on age. For example, where employers have attempted to justify less favourable treatment based on age by reference to customer preference this has not been accepted.[207]

In effect, courts have responded to the multi-dimensional aspect of age equality by fairly ready acceptance of labour market or structural aims as legitimate, whilst at the same time addressing the reliance on stereotypes and prejudicial assumptions related to age. This has at times led to a lack of consistency in the treatment of age discrimination. Examples include the fact that dignity arguments have been accepted as justifying compulsory retirement despite their reliance on inherent stereotypes regarding declining capacity with age; and the fairly ready acceptance of cost as a factor justifying differential treatment by age. This inconsistency reflects the difficulty inherent in reconciling the competing structural, economic and social elements at play in age equality cases.

Sweden

As with other northern European states, Sweden has an ageing population, and public policy aims to encourage longer working lives.[208] Although the focus of its anti-discrimination law has been to tackle barriers faced by older workers in order to meet the labour market demands of an ageing workforce, attention is also needed on counteracting youth unemployment.

Sweden's equality law, the Discrimination Act 2008, implements Equality Directive 2000/78, although the legislation was enacted two years after the 2006 deadline provided in the Directive. The 2008 Act covers seven grounds including age, and its age protection extends beyond the employment sphere to cover education and access to goods and services. Prior to this, there was no comprehensive protection against age discrimination, although a 1973 government regulation prohibited discrimination on the basis of sex or age in state employment.[209]

---

207 *O'Reilly v BBC and others* ET 22004223/2010.

208 B. Nyström, 'Active Ageing and Labour Law in Sweden' in F Hendrickx (ed.), *Active Ageing and Labour Law* (2012, Intersentia, Cambridge).

209 See L. Carlson, The Metamorphosis of Swedish Discrimination Law in K. Ahlberg, K. Källström, J. Malmberg, M. Koch (eds), *Vänbok till Ronnie Eklund* (Uppsala: Iustus, 2010) at p. 92.

In accordance with the Directive, the Swedish legislation protects against direct and indirect discrimination, harassment and victimization. Perceived discrimination, discrimination by association and instructions to discriminate are also prohibited. As with the EU directive, both direct and indirect age discrimination can be justified where proportionate. As well as the legislation governing age discrimination, it should be noted that Sweden has a highly unionised labour market, and collective agreements govern practice in many workplaces.[210]

Discrimination against Younger Workers

As elsewhere in EU, discrimination against younger workers is embedded in many labour market structures. Although pay and conditions of work are not provided by statute in Sweden, many collective agreements allow for differential terms based on age, such as pay rates. These might be seen to be *prima facie* breaches of the anti-discrimination principle, but are usually accepted as justified as protective of younger workers.[211] In addition, under the 1982 Employment Protection Act, a principle of seniority can apply in redundancy cases.[212] This tends to result in discrimination against younger workers who are less likely to have built up the longer years of service which can lead to redundancy protection, as well as increased redundancy payments.

In addition to less favourable treatment of younger workers, some more favourable treatment for older workers can also be readily justified. For example, two examples can be seen in the travaux préparatoires of legitimate aims that are likely to be treated as both appropriate and necessary. First, that better paid vacation conditions are justified because older workers need more rest than younger workers in order to be able to work until they retire; and second that better conditions regarding periods of notice for dismissals for older workers are also justified as an aid to help them work until retirement.[213] In addition,

210 J.J. Votinius, 'Age Discrimination and Labour Law in Sweden' in A. Numhauser-Henning and M. Rönnmar (eds), *Age Discrimination and Labour Law: Comparative and Conceptual Perspectives in the EU and Beyond* (Kluwer, The Netherlands, 2015).

211 J.J. Votinius, 'Age Discrimination and Labour Law in Sweden' in A. Numhauser-Henning and M. Rönnmar (eds), *Age Discrimination and Labour Law: Comparative and Conceptual Perspectives in the EU and Beyond* (Kluwer, The Netherlands, 2015).

212 Swedish 1982 Employment Protection Act section 22.

213 Per Norberg, Sweden: Country Report Non-Discrimination, European Network of Legal Experts in gender equality and non-discrimination (2017, European Commission).

collective agreements will often include rules on annual leave, redundancy pay etc. based on age.[214]

Discrimination against Older Workers

The use of age in redundancy can lead to greater protection for older workers, for example seniority schemes such as last in first out. However, as well the Employment Protection Act allowing for a principle of seniority to apply in redundancy cases, some redundancy schemes will also allow for redundancy selection to be based on age in conjunction with pension entitlement. This will lead to less favourable treatment for older workers who become more likely to be selected for redundancy as they have pension entitlement. However, where such schemes lead to compulsory redundancies they can be difficult to justify.

For example, in a case involving a redundancy situation for cabin crew[215] a collective agreement allowed the employer to dismiss all those over the age of 60, as they were entitled to a full pension within the employer's pension scheme. The employer sought to justify the age discrimination involved in selecting those over 60 for redundancy on the basis that they had a right to a full pension; that there were legitimate social reasons to choose them for dismissal, namely to distribute employment fairly between generations; and to ensure that the remaining employees were not all close to the pensionable age. However, the Labour Court held that the same aims could be achieved through a voluntary redundancy scheme, and so compulsory redundancy for those over 60 was not proportionate.

Retirement

Sweden has no state mandatory retirement age, although employers can impose retirement at 67 years. Thus employers are allowed to terminate employment for employees with one month's notice when they reach the age of 67. The lawfulness of this provision was confirmed by the CJEU in *Hörnfeldt v Meddelande* and the aims of avoiding humiliating dismissals of older workers, adapting to demographic change, and the need to help younger workers enter the labour market were accepted as legitimate.[216]

However, although employers are able to compulsorily retire staff when they reach 67, relying on the labour market justifications identified and confirmed in *Hörnfeldt*, this does not mean that all dismissals from the age of 67

214 B. Nyström, 'Active Ageing and Labour Law in Sweden' in F. Hendrickx (ed.), *Active Ageing and Labour Law* (2012, Intersentia, Cambridge).

215 Labour Court case 2011 No. 37,225

216 Case C-141/11 Judgment of the CJEU 5 July 2012.

onwards will be lawful. Instead, once the employee has passed the age of 67, the legal position reverts to require that any age discrimination be justified. This was confirmed in *Keolis*,[217] where the employer legally dismissed bus drivers at the age of 67 and re-hired them on a fixed short-term hourly basis. This re-employment was not renewed after the age of 70. The court treated non-renewal as direct age discrimination: the exception allowing dismissal at the age of 67 only applied at the age of 67, and not beyond.[218] Any further age discrimination therefore remained to be justified.

Intersectionality

Swedish anti-discrimination legislation does not specifically cover multiple discrimination. Moreover, although courts have accepted that two grounds of discrimination can arise in a single case, the fact that one incident gave rise to two grounds of discrimination did not give rise to additional compensation. One example is where an employer discriminated on grounds of age and sex by failing to call an older woman to a job interview. Although the employer claimed that the woman was not suitable for the job, there was insufficient evidence to refute the presumption of age discrimination and sex discrimination.[219] Although the Labour Court recognised that both grounds of discrimination had occurred, this was not seen as reason to increase the damages award.[220]

Conclusion on Age Discrimination in Sweden

Sweden's late adoption of age discrimination laws, together with its broad acceptance of exceptions to the principle of equality when it comes to age discrimination, illustrates again the difficulties that courts face when implementing age equality protection. The tension between meeting structural challenges of an ageing workforce, balancing the interests of different age groups, and upholding equal dignity and respect for all workers is illustrated in the broader exceptions that are allowed for age discrimination than for other equality grounds. In addition, the failure of the Labour Court to

217 Labour Court, Case 2015 no 51, the Equality Ombudsman v. Keolis AB (judgment of 16.09.2015).

218 The position can be contrasted with the situation in South Africa.

219 (Labour Court 2010 No 91, The Equality Ombudsman v. State Employment Board (Statens arbetsgivarverk) (judgment of 15.12.2010).)

220 J.J. Votinius, 'Intersectionality as a Tool for Analysing Labour Law' in S. Manfredi and L. Vickers (ed.), *Challenges of Active Ageing: Equality Law and the Workplace*, Palgrave Macmillan UK (2016).

recognise intersectional discrimination, in particular the cumulative impact of age with gender, is identified by Votinius as a limitation of the Swedish anti-discrimination framework.[221]

Despite a strong social and legislative commitment to equality in general in Sweden, age discrimination is embedded in many of the labour market structures, such as wage setting, seniority systems for redundancy, and annual leave entitlements and the acceptance of retirement at the age of 67. The somewhat contradictory approach of the legislature and the courts in tackling age discrimination, with their fairly ready justification for age discriminatory practices, reflects the complicated relationship between the economic and social aspects of age equality, discussed in Part 1.

US

The US has one of the earliest non-discrimination laws specifically relating to age: the 1967 Age Discrimination in Employment Act (ADEA). The ADEA protects against age discrimination against those over 40, making it unlawful to

> fail or refuse to hire or to discharge any individual or otherwise discriminate against any individual with respect to his compensation, terms, conditions, or privileges of employment, because of such individual's age; to limit, segregate, or classify his employees in any way which would deprive or tend to deprive any individual of employment opportunities or otherwise adversely affect his status as an employee, because of such individual's age.[222]

The ADEA was introduced soon after, and modelled on, the protection of other equality grounds under Title VII of the Civil Rights Act 1964. The ADEA protects against disparate treatment and disparate impact based on age (i.e. direct and indirect discrimination), as well as protecting against harassment and retaliation for opposing or challenging age discrimination.[223] Discriminatory treatment may be conscious or may be the result of the application of

221 J.J. Votinius, 'Intersectionality as a Tool for Analysing Labour Law' in S. Manfredi and L. Vickers (ed.), *Challenges of Active Ageing: Equality Law and the Workplace*, Palgrave Macmillan UK (2016).

222 Age Discrimination in Employment Act 1967 29 U.S.C. § 623(a) (1), (2).

223 For a discussion of the US law, see G. Lester, 'Age Discrimination and Labor Law in the United States' in A. Numhauser-Henning and M. Rönnmar (eds), *Age Discrimination and Labour Law: Comparative and Conceptual Perspectives in the EU and Beyond* (Kluwer, The Netherlands, 2015).

stereotypical assumptions. Claims that an employer's action was motivated by age are known as disparate treatment claims. In addition, the Supreme Court has accepted claims based on disparate impact, where employment practices or polices are facially neutral, but have a disproportionately adverse impact on older workers.[224] The ADEA does not formally define age discrimination in separate terms (unlike the EU framework in which direct and indirect discrimination are defined separately) but the Supreme Court has accepted claims based on both disparate impact and disparate treatment.[225]

In addition to the ADEA, many individual states have their own laws prohibiting age discrimination, some of which predate the introduction of the 1967 ADEA.[226] In what follows, the focus is on the ADEA as it applies in all states and to all employers with over 20 employees.

As with the EU, the US has an ageing population and the law has been developed in this context.[227] The introduction of the ADEA followed the 1965 Wirtz Report which had found substantial evidence of arbitrary age discrimination in the workplace.[228] Unlike the law in other countries, which is included in a general equality framework, the US age discrimination law does not promote age equality in general, but is limited to prohibiting discrimination against older workers.

Discrimination against Younger Workers

The ADEA only applies to those over 40, and there are no federal laws protecting against age discrimination in general which could be used to protect younger worker against either structural inequalities or prejudicial or stereotyped assumptions about their abilities.

Even if applicants are over 40 themselves, the ADEA does not protect them if they are treated less favourably than those of an older age, only if treated less favourably than those who are younger. For example, in *General Dynamics*

224 *Smith v City of Jackson*, 544 U.S. 228 (2005).

225 M. Horan, 'The Supreme Court Retires Disparate Impact: Kentucky Retirement Systems v. EEOC Validates the Disparate Treatment Theory under the Age Discrimination in Employment Act' (2009) 29 J. Nat'l Ass'n Admin. L. Judiciary 115.

226 M. Horan, 'The Supreme Court Retires Disparate Impact: Kentucky Retirement Systems v. EEOC Validates the Disparate Treatment Theory under the Age Discrimination in Employment Act' (2009) 29 J. Nat'l Ass'n Admin. L. Judiciary 115.

227 J.Z. Rothenberg, D.S. Gardner 'Protecting Older Workers: The Failure of the Age Discrimination in Employment Act of 1967' (2011) 38(1) *Journal of Sociology and Social Welfare* 9.

228 W.W. Wirtz, The Older American Worker: Age Discrimination in Employment, Report of the Secretary of Labor to the Congress under Section 715 of the Civil Rights Act of 1964, (1965).

Land Systems v *Cline*[229] the firm provided additional health care benefits for employees who were over 50. A group of staff who were aged 40–49 claimed that this breached the ADEA: they were over 40 and so eligible to make a claim, and had been treated less favourably on grounds of age as they were not eligible for the additional benefits. Their claim was rejected on the basis that the ADEA does not prohibit preferential treatment for older people. The Court referred to the fact that its social context and legislative history show that it was aimed to protect older workers and was not intended to stop their more favourable treatment.

The lack of symmetry creates a significant limitation in the legal protection against age discrimination in the US,[230] as evidence suggests that age discrimination is experienced by younger workers as well as older workers.[231] Despite the fact that the law in the US was formulated to address stigmatising stereotype, which is experienced by young and old, its economic dimension becomes clear in the light of this restriction. The main aim of the age discrimination legislation was to promote the employment of older workers based on their abilities and so to prohibit the reliance on age based stereotypes in hiring decisions. Whilst the focus was on confronting stereotypes, the motivation was to address a particular economic issue, namely the difficulties caused by an ageing population: and this was to be achieved by removing hindrances to their retention and recruitment in the workplace.[232]

Discrimination against Older Workers

In order to establish an age discrimination claim, the worker must show that he or she is over 40 and qualified for the position in question; was adversely affected by being dismissed, demoted or not offered employment; and that someone similarly qualified but substantially younger was employed (or

229 540 U.S. 581, 593 (2004).

230 S. Bisom-Rapp and M. Sargeant, 'Diverging Doctrine, Converging Outcomes: Evaluating Age Discrimination Law in the United Kingdom and the United States' (2013) 44 *Loyola University Chicago Law Journal* 717 *available at* http://ssrn.com/abstract=2154327; S.M. Saldarriaga, 'Flaming Fifties and beyond: An International Comparison of Age Discrimination Laws and How the United States Could Improve the Laws for Elderly Women', (2017) 25 *Elder L.J.* 101.

231 See G. Lester, 'Age Discrimination and Labor Law in the United States' in A. Numhauser-Henning and M. Rönnmar (eds), *Age Discrimination and Labour Law: Comparative and Conceptual Perspectives in the EU and Beyond* (Kluwer, The Netherlands, 2015), 398.

232 S. Bisom-Rapp and M. Sargeant, 'Diverging Doctrine, Converging Outcomes: Evaluating Age Discrimination Law in the United Kingdom and the United States' (2013) 44 *Loyola University Chicago Law Journal* 717 *available at* http://ssrn.com/abstract=2154327.

retained) instead. Courts have varied in how much younger a comparator must be to count as 'substantially' younger, but in most cases the difference in age is expected to be at least 10 years.[233] The substantially younger person may be over 40, so for example a 56 year old who was replaced by a 40 year old could still claim age discrimination.[234]

Once a *prima facie* claim of age discrimination is established, the employer can defend the claim by pointing to a non-discriminatory reason for the treatment. If the employer is able to show an alternative reason for the adverse treatment, the employee may then refute this by showing that the employer's reason was a pretext, for example by showing a pattern of age related poor treatment. The US courts have been fairly ready to accept alternative reasons than age as explaining adverse treatment, including costs and other reasons that are fairly closely linked to age. For example, in *Hazen Paper Co. v Biggins*[235] an employer was able to establish alternative reasons for dismissing an employee, on the basis that he was close to the age when his pension entitlement would vest. The Court held that age must have had 'a determinative influence' on the employer's decision. Here the decision was motivated by factors other than age (the vesting of pension) and was not linked to the problem of inaccurate and stigmatizing stereotypes about older workers' productivity and competence, which was the wrong to which the ADEA was directed. The Court took the view that a decision based on years of service was analytically distinct from age.

The ADEA can give rise to disparate impact claims, where reliance on neutral rules have a disproportionately adverse impact on older workers.[236] In such cases, the employee has to establish a *prima facie* case of age discrimination by showing the disproportionate impact of a policy or practice, and the burden then shifts to the employer who may be able demonstrate that the policy or practice is based on a reasonable factor other than age. The Supreme Court has been clear that the standard of protection for age discrimination is lower than for other protected grounds, with the standard of review needed to show that a practice is 'reasonable', less stringent than the 'business necessity' test required to justify discrimination on other grounds protected in the USA

233 See *Nagle v Village of Calumet Park*, 554 F.3d 1106, 1118 (7th Cir. 2009) cited in G. Lester, 'Age Discrimination and Labor Law in the United States' in A. Numhauser-Henning and M. Rönnmar (eds), *Age Discrimination and Labour Law: Comparative and Conceptual Perspectives in the EU and Beyond* (Kluwer, The Netherlands, 2015).

234 *O'Connor v Consolidated Coin Caterers Corp.* 517 U.S. 308 (1996).

235 507 U.S. 604 (1993).

236 *Smith v City of Jackson*, 544 U.S. 228 (2005).

under Title VII. For example, those claiming age discrimination are not able to challenge the justifications put forward by the employer by showing that there are alternative less discriminatory practices that could achieve the same aim. Moreover, costs based justifications are likely to be accepted as reasonable.[237]

Exceptions

The ADEA provides a number of exceptions and defences to age discrimination claims. Certain seniority systems and employee benefits plans are protected under the Act.[238] In addition, exceptions apply allowing for maximum ages to be set for hiring of staff, and also allowing for the dismissal of police officers and firefighters at the age of 55.[239]

Age may also be a bona fide occupational requirement reasonably necessary to the normal operation of the business, or the less favourable treatment may be based on reasonable factors other than age.[240] The bona fide occupational requirement exception, together with the defence that the treatment was reasonably necessary for factors other than age, creates a fairly wide space for justifying age discrimination. Unlike the EU legal framework which limits the justification of direct age discrimination to reasons linked to broader employment policy,[241] under the ADEA, age discrimination can be justified for reasons that are particular to the individual business, including costs, which themselves may be age related.

The ease with which treatment can be justified when it is clearly age-related, albeit not directly based on age, represents a significant weakness in the protection for age discrimination in the US.

The Case of Retirement

The prohibition against age discrimination contained in the ADEA applies to retirement, making compulsory retirement unlawful.[242] There are some exceptions however: retirement is lawful in respect of staff in executive or high policy making positions over the age of 65. This exception is subject to the

237 M.C. Harper, 'Reforming the Age Discrimination in Employment Act: Proposals and Prospects', (2012)16 Emp. Rts. & Emp. Pol'y J. 13.

238 29 U.S.C. § 623(f) (2) (A)–(B). These are rarely likely to be challenged, as most seniority schemes treat older workers more favourably than younger workers, and so do not discriminate against older workers.

239 29 U.S.C. § 623(j).

240 29 U.S.C. § 623(f) (1).

241 Cross refer to EU law section.

242 Originally the ADEA only applied to those aged 40–65. The upper age limit was raised to 70 and then removed entirely in 1987.

proviso that the employee must have been employed for the two years in the high ranking position immediately prior to retirement and must be entitled to a pension or equivalent of at least $44,000 a year.[243]

Although compulsory retirement for most employees would amount to age discrimination, this does not prevent other action to encourage retirement. For example, early retirement incentive programmes are lawful, as long as they are voluntary and offered to reduce costs.[244] However, the 1990 Older Worker Benefit Protection Act imposes strict procedural requirements on employers who incentivise older workers into retirement.[245]

The exclusion of high level policy making roles from the ban on retirement creates an interesting tension within the ADEA. One rationale for this exception is given by Lester, as allowing employers to replace key employees and keep promotional channels open to younger employees.[246] Some element of intergenerational fairness is thus recognized within the ADEA's prohibition on retirement, albeit limited to a small number of high level appointments. This concern for promotion for younger colleagues, taken with the requirement for a healthy retirement income before mandatory retirement can be allowed, as well as the limit to high level executives, shows the US system reflecting some of the concerns regarding age equality discussed in Part 1. The dual role of employment as having an economic as well as an expressive function is reflected in the rules. The minimum pension requirement demonstrates a regard for the important economic function of work in individual lives and a concern to avoid individual disadvantage. The requirement for two years' prior experience in the role signals a recognition that individuals gain personal fulfilment from work, and may want to have a reasonable innings in a particular high level and probably rewarding role. Moreover, an alternative rationale, based on the difficulty in measuring performance objectively, and the emotional distress that may be created in the process suggests that broader dignity based arguments also account for the exception for high level executives.[247]

---

243 29 U.S.C. § 631 (c) (1).

244 29 U.S.C. § 623(f)(2)(B)(ii), added to ADEA in 1990 under the Older Workers' Benefit Protection Act.

245 S. Bisom-Rapp and M. Sargeant, 'Diverging Doctrine, Converging Outcomes: Evaluating Age Discrimination Law in the United Kingdom and the United States' (2013) 44 *Loyola University Chicago Law Journal* 717 *available at* http://ssrn.com/abstract=2154327.

246 G. Lester, 'Age Discrimination and Labor Law in the United States' in A. Numhauser-Henning and M. Rönnmar (eds), *Age Discrimination and Labour Law: Comparative and Conceptual Perspectives in the EU and Beyond* (Kluwer, The Netherlands, 2015).

247 R. Doty, 'Age Discrimination in Employment Act and Mandatory Retirement of Law Firm Partners (1979–80) 53 S. Cal. L. Rev. 1679, cited in A.L. Goldman 'Age Discrimination

However, the recognition of more social aims of equality law, including the concern for intergenerational justice, is only very partial under the ADEA and it could be remarked that promotional channels are of equal value to younger staff even when not involving promotion to high level policy making jobs. The group protected here seems to be those in line for the high level jobs, rather than those with perhaps more modest but no less important personal ambitions.

The general prohibition on retirement in the US has led to some noteworthy developments from an age equality perspective. Whilst staff do not have to retire, nonetheless the structural needs of the labour market, identified in the EU context as 'legitimate aims' for imposing retirement, still continue, with a need for employment opportunities for younger workers. The fact that retirement cannot be used to meet these needs can be identified as a shortcoming of the US legal framework. One response by employers has been the introduction of incentives to retire, which are exempted from age discrimination protection. This can be framed as an additional benefit for older workers who become eligible not only to pension income but also to additional compensation for taking up that income, and as such, these practices can be said to lead to double benefits for older workers at the expense of younger workers.

Intersectionality

The ADEA does not provide for dual or combined discrimination. Unlike other discrimination grounds under the equality provisions of Title VII, in which mixed motive cases can be allowed, under the ADEA those claiming age discrimination must show that age was the determinative factor for the adverse treatment. The fact that the ADEA does not accept mixed motives age discrimination claims was confirmed in *Gross v FBL Financial Services* in 2009.[248] As a result, the ADEA has not been able effectively to tackle the existence of intersectional and multiple discrimination faced by older women.[249] Indeed, studies have shown that the majority of successful age discrimination cases have been brought by men, dismissed from white-collar or managerial positions.[250]

Law—A Perspective from the USA' in F. Hendrickx (ed.) *Active Ageing and Labour Law* (2012, Intersentia, Cambridge).

248 557 U.S. 167 (2009).

249 S.M. Saldarriaga, 'Flaming Fifties and beyond: An International Comparison of Age Discrimination Laws and How the United States Could Improve the Laws for Elderly Women', (2017) 25 *Elder L.J.* 101.

250 J.Z. Rothenberg, D.S. Gardner, 'Protecting Older Workers: The Failure of the Age Discrimination in Employment Act of 1967' (2011) 38(1) *Journal of Sociology and Social*

Moreover, the provision of age equality legislation separate from other equality laws makes the creation of dual claims more problematic as standards of protection vary. For example, where business interests are used to justify disparate impact claims the tests differ, with economic necessity required for Title VII claims involving other equality protected characteristics, and only reasonable economic needs for age equality cases.

Conclusion on Age Discrimination in the USA

The introduction of the Age Discrimination in Employment Act 1967 will certainly have had an effect on age equality in the US labour market, and employment practices will undoubtedly have been changed on the ground. For example, one result is the removal of age limits in job adverts;[251] and the Act has been effective in protecting workers who are already in employment.[252]

Nonetheless, what is clear from this overview of the age discrimination law in the US is that the legal framework contains some significant limitations. The first distinctive feature of the US law is its asymmetry, and the lack of protection for younger workers, something that stands in marked contrast to other jurisdictions. Second, although the US age equality framework contains fewer formal exemptions than the parallel protection in other jurisdictions,[253] the standard of protection remains weak and age discrimination is treated as less serious than discrimination based on other protected characteristics. For example, the Supreme Court has repeatedly refused to extend the same level of scrutiny in cases under the ADEA as that applied under Title VII;[254] and the decision in *Gross v FBL Financial Services*[255] that age must be a but-for cause for any less favourable treatment significantly limits the effectiveness of the

---

Welfare 9; G. Rutherglen, 'From Race to Age: the Expanding Scope of Employment Discrimination Law (1995) 24(2) *The Journal of Legal Studies* 491.

251 D. Neumark, 'The Age Discrimination in Employment Act and the Challenge of Population Aging,' (2009) 31 (1) *Research on Aging* 41–68.

252 S.M. Saldarriaga, 'Flaming Fifties and beyond: An International Comparison of Age Discrimination Laws and How the United States Could Improve the Laws for Elderly Women', (2017) 25 *Elder L.J.* 101.

253 For example, there is no exception for retirement, and social and labour policy is not listed as grounds for exceptions to disparate treatment claims (or direct discrimination to use the EU terminology).

254 Smith v. City of Jackson 544 U.S. 228 (2005), discussed in M.C. Harper, 'Reforming the Age Discrimination in Employment Act: Proposals and Prospects', (2012) 16 Emp. Rts. & Emp. Pol'y J. 13.

255 557 U.S. 167 (2009).

protection available.[256] The 'reasonable factor other than age' defence makes it relatively easy for employers to defend cases.

The protection for age equality in the US is thus somewhat contradictory. One contradiction can be seen in the ADEA's promise of significant protection, which is then undermined by allowing fairly ready defences in age discrimination claims. A second contradiction can be seen in the bar on retirement, whilst allowing both an exception for high level executives and more generally applicable incentives to retire. These exceptions are likely to create additional advantage for those who are already more advantaged in socio-economic terms: either by creating additional compensation as people are given an incentive to retire; or by opening up jobs for the next generation, but only those who will step into the newly vacated well-paid high level jobs. These contradictions reflect the tension existing between the competing dimensions of age equality law discussed in Part 1. On the one hand, the ADEA was framed as a response to adverse age based stereotyping, which might suggest that it is underpinned by a concern for the social disadvantages of age discrimination. On the other hand, the fact that its protection is limited to discrimination against older workers suggests that its rationale is economic and structural: the reason for removing reliance on stereotype is not so much to address the stigmatic or expressive effects of stereotypes, but rather their economic effects.

Canada

The legal protection against age discrimination in Canada is provided within the federal legal system. All provinces, municipal and federal governments are subject to the Canadian Charter of Rights and Freedoms that contains an equality clause, which includes the right to equal protection and equal benefit of the law without discrimination based on age. The federal Canadian Human Rights Act, which applies to federally-regulated activities and entities, prohibits age discrimination and includes exceptions where age is a bona fide occupational requirement.[257] The Act goes on to provide that for the bona fide occupational requirement justification to be made out, it must be established that accommodation of the needs of an individual or a class of individuals affected would impose undue hardship on the person who would have to accommodate those needs, considering health, safety and cost.[258] In addition

256 J.J. Glenn and K.E. Little, 'A Study of the Age Discrimination in Employment Act of 1967' (2014) 31 GPSolo 41.

257 Canadian Human Rights Act s15(1).

258 Canadian Human Rights Act s 15(2). See P. Alon-Shenker, 'The Duty to Accommodate Senior Workers: Its Nature, Scope and Limitations' (2012) 38 Queen's LJ 165.

there are exceptions where employment is refused or terminated because the individual has not reached the minimum age, or has reached the maximum age that applies to that employment by law.[259] Mandatory retirement was allowed under the Canadian Human Rights Act, but this was abolished by the Government in 2011.

As well as equality provisions under the Charter and the Canadian Human Rights Act, each province has its own equality provisions contained in the legislation of the relevant province. To take two examples, in Ontario the Human Rights Code[260] provides a right to equal treatment without discrimination on grounds of age in a range of fields such as the provision of services, accommodation and employment. It provides an exception where age is a reasonable and bona fide qualification because of the nature of the employment. The Manitoba Human Rights Code prohibits age discrimination, including within its discrimination definition a right to reasonable accommodation, and contains an exception for bona fide and reasonable requirements or qualifications for the employment or occupation.[261]

All provinces prohibit age discrimination but while accommodation requirements may seem to vary, the requirement to consider accommodation is implied: an occupational requirement is unlikely to be bona fides if no reasonable accommodation has been made; and where the exception is framed in more general terms of a 'reasonable and justifiable' defence, the question of whether there was an attempt to accommodate may to be relevant to the question of justification. That is, the *Meiorin* case[262] clarified that in both direct and indirect cases of discrimination, to satisfy the bona fide occupational requirement, the employer has to show that it had attempted to accommodate to a point of undue hardship.

Discrimination against Younger Workers

Although the Canadian Human Rights Act protects generally against age discrimination, it provides an exception where an individual has not reached the minimum age for a job. Some provinces, such as Ontario and Alberta limit the protection of age discrimination to those over 18. Others, such as Manitoba do not have such a limitation.

---

259 Canadian Human Rights Act s15(1). Additional age related exceptions apply regarding terms and conditions of pensions funds.

260 Ontario Human Rights Code, R.S.O 1990, c. H. 19.

261 Manitoba Human Rights Code C.C.S.M. c. H175.

262 See *British Columbia (Public Service Employee Relations Comm) v BCGEU* [1999] 3 SCR 3 ('Meiorin').

In relation to discrimination against younger workers, a number of cases have arisen under the Canadian Charter of Rights and Freedoms relating to eligibility for various benefits, which have been based on age. Whilst they do not relate to employment, these illustrate some of the complexities courts have faced in determining age related cases.

The first case is *Law v Canada*[263] in which a woman who had been widowed under the age of 30 was not eligible for survivor's benefits under the Canadian Pension Plan. Eligibility was determined by age, with those over 45 eligible for a full pension benefit, and a tapering level of benefit for those aged 35–45, and no benefit for those under 35. Law claimed that this was discriminatory on grounds of age under the Charter. The Supreme Court found that it was not discriminatory. It held that any equality analysis under the Charter had to be purposive and contextual: it needed to consider whether the different treatment that arose here had a purpose and effect that was discriminatory, in particular whether withholding the benefit reflected the use of stereotypes or had the effect of 'perpetuating or promoting the view that the individual is less capable or worthy of recognition or value as a human being or as a member of Canadian society, equally deserving of concern, respect, and consideration.' The Supreme Court took the view that in this case, the refusal of the benefit to younger widows was not based on negative stereotypes, and did not reflect that younger women were held as of less value or deserving of less concern, respect or consideration. Indeed, the Court specified that adults under the age of 45 have not been consistently subjected to discrimination. The rules did not have the effect of violating the dignity of younger people, but were aimed at helping older widows and widowers meet their basic needs in the longer term. Indeed, the aim was to help overcome some of the age discrimination that can be faced by older workers who may face difficulty finding or maintaining employment as they age.

The decision in *Law* reflects many of the limitations of a dignity based approach to approaching age equality outlined in Part 1 above. The fact that age does not identify a 'discrete and insular minority' nor does it link to historical disadvantage, weighed against its protection in this instance.

This approach was followed in *Gosselin v. Québec*[264] which involved a social assistance scheme which paid those under 30 about one third of the amount paid to those of 30 or over. Those under 30 could increase their payment by participating in specified education or work experience programmes. This was challenged as a breach of the Canadian Charter of Rights and Freedoms, and

263 [1999] 1 SCR 497.

264 [2002] 4 SCR 429.

the Quebec Charter of Human Rights and Freedoms. The Supreme Court held that the Charters were not breached. Following the reasoning from *Law* the Court pointed out that younger people did not have any pre-existing disadvantage, stigmatisation or history of being undervalued; the aim of the different treatment corresponded to the actual need of younger people, having been designed to integrate them into the workforce; and the impact was not to undermine human dignity.

The decision was not unanimous, and a minority took an opposing view, pointing out that young people were disadvantaged by the lack of jobs available, that the law was based on an assumption that young people needed punitive measure to encourage the take up of training opportunities, and that the low level of benefits risked pushing young people into deep poverty. This meant that making their receipt of benefits conditional on undertaking further activity did undermine their dignity.

That the same facts led to such different opinions within the Supreme Court illustrates the difficulty courts can have in assessing equality claims in relation to age. Even though both the majority and minority agreed on the principles that should guide their decision, such as a concern to uphold dignity and redress disadvantage, different judges reached opposing conclusions when applying these principles to the facts.

The use of the somewhat vague concept of dignity in these cases has been criticised by many scholars,[265] and in the later case of *R. v Kapp*[266] the requirement introduced in *Law* that equality claims need to show lack of dignity was removed. The case did not involve age discrimination, but rather an affirmative action programme aimed at aboriginal groups. In assessing whether s15 of the Charter was infringed, the Supreme Court returned to a two stage test focused on whether there is discrimination on a prohibited ground and then on whether the treatment had the effect of perpetuating disadvantage or prejudice or was based on stereotyping. Although the concept of dignity can still be used, it no longer forms a separate part of the legal test of whether there has been unlawful discrimination.[267] Instead, other factors could indicate disadvantage in a particular case.

---

265 See for example, See R. O'Connell, The role of dignity in equality law; lessons from Canada and South Africa (2008) 6(2) International J. Constitutional law 267; S. Fredman, 'Substantive Equality Revisited' (2016) 14(3) International Journal of Constitutional Law 712.

266 [2008] 2 SCR 483.

267 Kapp ibid. at para 21.

Although the legal test used in *Law* and *Gosselin* has been amended in later cases, there is no suggestion that the simpler test set out in *Kapp* would lead to a different outcome in those cases. The cases illustrate the difficulty in demonstrating that unlawful discrimination against younger people has occurred, given that they are not recognised as a disadvantaged group. The focus on disadvantage and dignity in the Canadian case law, rather than a focus on differential treatment *per se* results in limited protection for younger people from unequal treatment. Although the cases have not involved differential treatment of younger workers, they suggest that where different treatment such as reduced employment rights is aimed at encouraging the employment of younger workers, it will be justified, even if it involves less favourable terms and conditions.

Discrimination against Older Workers

As well as providing an exception where an individual has not reached the minimum age for a job, the Canadian Human Rights Act also contains an exception for maximum ages when provided to under law or other employment related regulation.

The provisions protecting against age discrimination will protect employees or prospective staff from discrimination based on stereotypes such as assumptions that they are not capable of developing new skills. However, despite the fact that age discrimination is protected as part of the general non-discrimination provisions, cases involving older workers have not always been successful. For example, discrimination needs to be on the basis of age, so that actions based on factors related to age, but which are not based on age *per se* may not lead to findings of discrimination. Thus, less favourable treatment that is based on pension status, or being over qualified, do not relate to age *per se*, and so may not lead to findings of age discrimination, and where age is the cause of less favourable treatment, cost can be accepted as a justification for the differential treatment.[268]

Moreover, the duty to accommodate age related needs does not create a stringent requirement to accommodate older workers. For example, in *Riddell v IBM Canada*,[269] an older worker was unsuccessful in claiming discrimination. Riddell was dismissed after 33 years of service following poor performance. He had been moved into administrative and clerical positions and had his performance monitored for some time before his dismissal, after having been offered

268 See P. Alon-Shenker, 'Legal Barriers to Age Discrimination in Hiring Complaints' (2016) 39 Dal LJ 289.

269 2009 HRTO 1454.

early retirement. The Ontario Human Rights Tribunal accepted the employer's position that the dismissal was due to a failure to meet performance standards that were imposed across the company and that this was not based on age, and his claim was dismissed. The case was treated as one of direct discrimination, but as Alon-Shenker argues, the case shows a reluctance by the Tribunal to impose much by way of an obligation on the employer to accommodate Riddell's needs. For example, it did not consider providing the additional training that Riddell might have needed due to his age. Alon-Shenker points out that the level of accommodation required differs from that required in disability cases, where special training to meet a disability need would be likely to be expected of an employer.

A second example of the ease with which indirect discrimination on grounds of age can be justified can be seen in the case of *Bastide v Canada Post Corp.*[270] Casual workers had to pass a manual dexterity test as part of the recruitment process for permanent positions. There was a statistically significant relationship between age and failure rates on the test, with the result that younger staff were promoted to permanent positions ahead of older staff. The Federal Court ruled that the test was necessary to assess basic skills and so was a bona fide requirement, and that if the test were not used, it would create undue hardship for the employer in organizing staffing and in increasing its training costs.

The Case of Retirement

Under section 15(1) of the Charter, age discrimination is unlawful, but the right is not absolute, as under section 1 of the Charter rights are subject to 'such reasonable limits prescribed by law as can be demonstrably justified in a free and democratic society'. Under this limitation, retirement provisions have been justified and found to be constitutionally permissible.[271] Moreover, when originally drafted, the Canadian Human Rights Act created an exception for retirement. However, in 2012, the Act was amended to prohibit mandatory retirement. Retirement can still be imposed but only where the employer can show that it is necessary as a bona fide occupational requirement.

Provincial human rights codes also prohibit mandatory retirement, although different provinces deal with retirement differently. As originally drafted, most human rights codes did not apply to those over 65, effectively creating a freedom for employers to require retirement at 65 by removing any cause of

270 [2006] 2 FCR 637, aff'd 2006 FCA 318, 365 NR 136, leave to appeal to SCC refused, 31732 (March 8, 2007).

271 K. Thornicroft, 'The Uncertain State of Mandatory Retirement in Canada' (2016) Labor Law Journal 397.

action for those over that age. Over time, all provinces have repealed their 'less than 65' limitation on human rights claims. However, the result has not been the abolition of mandatory retirement, as every jurisdiction has legislation allowing retirement for particular occupations (for example the judiciary), as well as either exceptions for bona fide pension and retirement plans,[272] or an exception for bona fide occupational requirements, or both.

Thus, although the legal mechanisms differ, the result is that blanket retirement rules would be unlawful, but individual incidents of retirement can be justified, albeit with differing levels of scrutiny required in different provinces and under different exceptions. For the exception related to pension and retirement plans to apply, retirement only needs to be genuinely part of such a scheme. In relation to the more general bona fide occupational requirement exception, the *Meiorin* test applies,[273] and retirement must be adopted in good faith, for a rational job-related purpose, and be reasonably necessary to accomplish that purpose. In addition, the employer must show that it would be impossible to accommodate individual employees adversely affected by the rule, policy or practice without imposing undue hardship on the employer. The *Meiorin* test has meant that routine retirement, in the absence of a retirement or pension plan, can be more difficult to justify. For example, In *Way v Department of Education*,[274] a bus driver was dismissed on reaching the age of 65 because of provincial regulations requiring retirement at that age for reasons of safety. Way successfully challenged the rule on the basis that it had not been shown that the rule was reasonably necessary for school bus safety: it had been imposed in a blanket way without any consideration for individual circumstances.

Thus, although clear protection against mandatory retirement exists in Canada, nonetheless, retirement can still be justified by employers, as long as reasons are provided and many Canadian employees are still made to retire.[275]

---

272 Around 84% of Canadian employees work in a jurisdiction which contains the exception for retirement or pension plans, although not every employer will have such a plan. K. Thornicroft, 'The Uncertain State of Mandatory Retirement in Canada' (2016) Labor Law Journal 397, 401.

273 See *British Columbia (Public Service Employee Relations Comm) v BCGEU* [1999] 3 SCR 3 ('Meiorin').

274 2011 CanLII 13074 (NBLEB).

275 K. Thornicroft, 'The Uncertain State of Mandatory Retirement in Canada' (2016) Labor Law Journal 397.

Intersectionality

The Canadian Human Rights Act does not explicitly allow for intersectional or multiple claims. As with other jurisdictions, where more than one ground of discrimination arises, claims would need to be brought on both grounds.

Conclusion on Age Discrimination in Canada

Canada is a jurisdiction with a long record of protecting against age discrimination with Charter protection dating from the 1980s, and other protection predating this.[276] Despite its relatively early adoption of protection for age equality, the courts still face many of the same difficulties existing in other jurisdictions that have later adopted age equality laws when it comes to balancing the needs of older and younger workers with the business needs of employers. Although the protection extends beyond that available in the EU and the US by including a duty of accommodation as well as the prohibition of discrimination, the Canadian courts have not used this additional aspect of its equality framework to create extensive protection for age equality in the workplace, and the challenge remains to balance dignity and respect for workers regardless of age, with the structural needs of the workplace. Instead of taking a strong, age inclusive approach, a relatively low standard of review is set and age discrimination can be fairly readily justified. The failure of the Canadian framework to create a strong framework to protect dignified lives is identified by Alon-Shenker as a particular limitation of the Canadian age discrimination framework, together with its lack of recognition of the intersection between age and disability.[277] Again, the case law reflects the complicated relationship between the economic and social aspects of age equality, discussed in Part 1. In particular, the Canadian cases illustrate the way in which arguments based on dignity can work in unpredictable ways in relation to discrimination against younger people, with the fact that young people do not have a long history of being undervalued being used to justify age discriminatory practices, despite their adverse impact on particular disadvantaged young people.

---

276 For example in Ontario protection existed for those age 40 to 64 (see Ontario Age Discrimination Act 1966).

277 P. Alon-Shenker, 'The Unequal Right to Age Equality: Towards a *Dignified Lives Approach* to Age Discrimination' (2012) XXV (2) *Canadian Journal of Law and Jurisprudence* 243; P. Alon-Shenker 'The Duty to Accommodate Senior Workers: Its Nature, Scope and Limitations' (2012) 38 Queen's LJ 165.

South Africa

In terms of age equality, the demographics of South Africa differ from the demographics in other states considered above, as it has a youthful population and unemployment for young people is significantly higher than for older people.[278] This means that the economic and structural issues influencing labour market policy differ, with intergenerational conflict being a particularly current issue.

South Africa has a progressive Constitution, which contains a strong commitment to equality. Section 9 of the Bill of Rights contains a fundamental right to equality on a wide ranging set of grounds including age.[279] As well as reflecting structural and economic imperatives, the Bill of Rights also reflects the social dimensions of age equality. Section 9 prohibits unfair discrimination and the Constitutional Court has made clear that in assessing whether a particular incident of discrimination is unfair, regard should be had to the role of human dignity.[280] In addition to the Constitutional protection for equality, age discrimination is covered in the equality legislation. The Labour Relations Act 1995 prohibits unfair labour practices including age discrimination with an exception of where otherwise discriminatory treatment is based on the inherent needs of the job, or if it is based on age and the employee had reached the normal retirement age. *Schweitzer v Waco Distributors (A division of Voltex (Pty) Ltd)*[281] confirms that once an employee reaches normal retirement age, any subsequent dismissal based on age will be lawful.

The Employment Equity Act 1998 also prohibits discrimination on grounds of age. It too includes exceptions based on the inherent needs of the job, as well as an exception for affirmative action. The effect of the Employment Equity Act and the Labour Relations Act is that age discrimination is protected through the prohibition of direct and indirect discrimination on grounds including age, as well as harassment on grounds of age. Two defences exist

---

278 Quarterly Labour Force Survey—QLFS Q3:2017, available at http://www.statssa.gov.za/?page_id=1854&PPN=P0211 accessed 11 January 2018.

279 N. Smit, 'Age Discrimination and Labor Law in South Africa: Intersectional and Intergenerational Challenges' in A. Numhauser-Henning and M. Rönnmar (eds), *Age Discrimination and Labour Law: Comparative and Conceptual Perspectives in the EU and Beyond* (Kluwer, The Netherlands, 2015). See also S. Fredman, Comparative study of anti-discrimination and equality laws of the US, Canada, South Africa and India, European Network of Legal Experts in the non-discrimination field (2012) available at http://ec.europa.eu/justice/discrimination/files/comparative_study_ad_equality_laws_of_us_canada_sa_india_en.pdf (accessed 17 January 2018).

280 *President of RSA v Hugo* 1997 6 BCLR 708 (CC).

281 (1998) 19 ILJ 1573.

under the Employment Equality Act 1998: affirmative action and discrimination which is linked to the inherent needs of the job. The acceptance of retirement under the Labour Relations Act acts as an additional exception to non-discrimination prohibition,[282] as employers can justify dismissal on the basis that retirement age has been reached.[283]

Equality law in general is well developed in South Africa, with strong protections in employment law and under the Constitution, largely in response to the recent history of apartheid with its institutionalised and systematic racial discrimination. Although the equality framework is not limited to race discrimination, the significant challenge of tackling race discrimination has meant that the case law relating to age discrimination is not as well developed.

Moreover, the particular imperative to create a more diverse workforce, together with demographic challenges of under- and unemployment among young people, especially black young people, has meant that age related employment practices have not been prohibited. For example, age-related discrimination is accepted as lawful in cases such as 'last in first out' redundancy arrangements. Whilst use of age per se would not be accepted as a criterion for redundancy, age related LIFO practices are accepted as objective and fair.[284]

The Case of Retirement

A mandatory retirement age is not unlawful in South Africa. This perhaps reflects the greater concern for the creation of jobs for younger workers, given the very high unemployment rates among young people. In addition, retirement can also be justified as a mechanism to promote diversity in the future

---

282 *HOSPERSA on behalf of Venter v SA Nursing Council* (2006) 27 ILJ 1143 (LC) the Labour Court effectively read into the EEA the exceptions in LRA on age discrimination claims from those over retirement age.

283 See C. Garbers, 'Discriminatory Dismissal' in EML Strydom (ed.) *Essential Employment Discrimination Law* (2012 Juta, Claremont) and C. Bosch 'Age Discrimination in South African Labour Law: A Critical Assessment of the Law on 'retiring' Older Workers' in O. Dupper and C. Garbers (eds) *Equality in the Workplace: Reflections from South Africa and Beyond* (2009) *Juta and Co. Ltd, Cape Town*) for discussion of the case law on how to establish normal and agreed retirement ages.

284 Screenex Wire Weaving Manufacturing (Pty) Ltd Ngema and Others (2010) 31 ILJ 2607 (LC), cited in N. Smit, 'Age Discrimination and Labor Law in South Africa: Intersectional and Intergenerational Challenges' in A. Numhauser-Henning and M. Rönnmar (eds), *Age Discrimination and Labour Law: Comparative and Conceptual Perspectives in the EU and Beyond* (Kluwer, The Netherlands, 2015).

workforce, as older, white, staff are replaced by younger people from more diverse backgrounds.[285]

Intersectionality

Given its apartheid history, it is not surprising that South Africa has a particular concern for intersectional equality. Access to employment varies by racial group, with Black Africans at a particular disadvantage. Looking at the intersection of race and age, elderly Black Africans experience the highest levels of poverty.[286] The South African Constitutional Court has accepted intersectional discrimination claims, although none of the cases have involved age as one of the grounds.[287]

Conclusion on Age Discrimination in South Africa

The history, social context and demographics of South Africa differ from those of many other states with legal provisions governing age equality, with its history of deep and entrenched race inequality, as well as a youthful demographic. Yet, despite these differences, as with other states, the law relating to age discrimination in South Africa has had to address the tensions discussed in Part 1, between maintaining the essential dignity of different groups of workers by prohibiting discrimination based on stereotype and prejudicial assumptions on the one hand, and utilising the labour market as a tool to redress economic and structural disadvantage faced by particular groups on the other.

In South Africa, whilst legislation exists creating a framework to address less favourable treatment based on stereotypical views related to age, the balance between the two limbs of equality has largely been struck in favour of using age discrimination law to address structural and economic aims of equality. In particular, the structural labour market mechanisms such as compulsory retirement have been maintained, in part as a way to promote diversity, on age and other grounds, elsewhere in the labour market.

---

285 N. Smit, 'Age Discrimination and Labor Law in South Africa: Intersectional and Intergenerational Challenges' in A. Numhauser-Henning and M. Rönnmar (eds), *Age Discrimination and Labour Law: Comparative and Conceptual Perspectives in the EU and Beyond* (Kluwer, The Netherlands, 2015).

286 N Smit, 'Age Discrimination and Labor Law in South Africa: Intersectional and Intergenerational Challenges' in A Numhauser-Henning and M Rönnmar (eds), *Age Discrimination and Labour Law: Comparative and Conceptual Perspectives in the EU and Beyond* (Kluwer, The Netherlands, 2015).

287 For example, *Bhe v Khayelitsha Magistrate* (CCT 49/03) [2004] ZACC 17; 2005 (1) SA 580 (CC); 2005 (1) BCLR 1 (CC) (South African Constitutional Court), in which the court accepted that the discrimination was on grounds of race and gender combined.

Part 3: Conclusion

A number of challenges involved in tackling age discrimination were identified in Part 1, ranging from significant societal change in economic and demographic terms, to a lack of conceptual clarity regarding the aims of equality law in the context of age. Part 2's comparative review of age discrimination in a range of jurisdictions confirms that these challenges are indeed reflected in the legal approaches taken to age equality. Although some differences can be identified, such as the different economic and demographic factors in South Africa, and the fact that the US protection only applies to older workers, the general picture arising from the comparison is instead one of common themes: all jurisdictions are clear in their rejection of prejudices and stigma related to age; all courts give some recognition to the structural dimensions to age equality by adopting a fairly low level of review of justification in age discrimination cases; most (with the exception of South Africa) view compulsory retirement as prima facie discriminatory, although here again the social and economic dimensions of age equality are reflected in the various exceptions through which retirement can be justified. Moreover, court decisions can be found in a number of jurisdictions that reflect the paradox of relying on dignity as an aim of age equality law, given its capacity to act as both a foundation for, and a limit on, the protection of age equality. The overarching theme that can be drawn from the comparative review, then, is that there is a lack of strong and coherent approach to tackling age equality internationally across the jurisdictions, with examples in each state of courts struggling to reconcile the competing demands of the economic, structural and social dimensions of age equality.

Rejection of Stereotyping and Prejudice

All courts have been clear that discrimination based on stigma and prejudicial stereotypes is unlawful. For example, the CJEU in *Petersen*[288] did not accept as legitimate the aim of avoiding the decline in dentists' performance after the age of 68 as this aim was based on a stereotype. Similarly, in Canada, in *Way v Department of Education*,[289] the mandatory retirement of bus drivers at 65 for reasons of safety was challenged because it had been imposed in a blanket way without any consideration for individual circumstances.

Moreover, good evidence is needed to justify any less favourable treatment based on an assumption that performance changes with age. So for example in *Wolf*[290] the discriminatory rules on starting work were justified as evidence

288 Case C-341/08.

289 2011 CanLII 13074 (NBLEB).

290 Case C-229/08.

was produced of a reduced operational capacity over the age of 50; and in *Bastide v Canada Post Corp.*[291] the use of manual dexterity tests as part of the recruitment process was justified despite its correlation with poorer performance for older workers: the manual dexterity was necessary to the job.

Standard of Review

Although most states are fairly strong in rejecting reliance on stereotypes to justify age discriminatory practices, the standard of review of justification in age cases is often lower than for other forms of discrimination. In the case of the US, this lower standard of review has been recognised explicitly, as the standard of review needed to show that a practice is 'reasonable' is less stringent than the 'business necessity' test required to justify discrimination on grounds under Title VII. The low level of review in the US is also seen in cases where the courts have accepted that the cause of the treatment was not age but eligibility for pension,[292] something which is technically a separate cause, but which is intimately linked to age.

In the case of the EU member states, there is no formal recognition that different standards of review apply, but the case law does suggest that the review is less strict in age cases. For example, UK courts have allowed discrimination to be justified on the basis of cost when necessary to avoid a windfall pay-out to the claimant.[293] Other types of justification accepted in the EU also illustrate the relatively low level of review used in age cases. For example, *Georgiev*[294] accepted as a legitimate the aim of maintaining a mix of different generations in order to promote the quality of teaching and research at universities, and the aim of keeping a balance of ages was also accepted in *Fuchs and Kohler v Land Hessen.*[295] Although the reason for wanting a mix could be based on operational needs, it is difficult to imagine courts accepting that quality of service requires a mix of other protected characteristics, given the potential for such rules to act as proxy for prejudicial preferences by customers.

The reduced standard of review in age cases could be taken to reflect ambivalence on the part of courts towards addressing the age based practices that are embedded within labour market structures. Whilst this might be said to suggest a lack of understanding of the social dimension of age equality, a more generous explanation is that courts are reflecting the need to hold the social

291 [2006] 2 FCR 637, aff'd 2006 FCA 318, 365 NR 136, leave to appeal to SCC refused, 31732 (March 8, 2007).

292 *Hazen Paper Co. v Biggins* 507 U.S. 604 (1993).

293 *Her Majesty's Land Registry v Benson and others* UKEAT/0197/11/RN.

294 C-250/09 and C-268/09.

295 C-159/10 and C-160/10.

dimension and the economic dimensions of age equality in balance. On this view, the lower standard of review reflects the fact that in the case of age, and unlike the case of other equality strands such as race and gender, there are strong economic and structural arguments in favour of age based rules which counterbalance the strong social justice aspects to age equality.

Retirement and Intergenerational Justice

The case of retirement was discussed above to illustrate the complexity of the intersection of economic and social dimensions of age equality law. Demographic changes have led to strong, but contradictory economic claims: in favour of retaining retirement as means to address youth unemployment; and against retirement in order to extend working lives as a means to address the economic cost of longer lives. The contradictory positions regarding retirement are reflected between and within the approaches to retirement in different jurisdictions.

The formal positions as regards retirement vary, with South Africa retaining mandatory retirement, the EU allowing mandatory retirement where it is justified, and the US and Canada officially prohibiting mandatory retirement. Although the US and Canada allow for justification of mandatory retirement in some circumstances, the EU has accepted a wider range of justifications, including those based on the economic and labour market aspects of age equality. Thus the EU and UK courts have accepted that mandatory retirement can help create jobs for younger people, and so have accepted 'inter-generational justice' as a legitimate aim for mandatory retirement policies. In contrast, the Canadian approach to justification is based on the needs of a particular job, so that it would be more difficult for an employer to justify mandatory retirement on the basis that it will free up jobs for younger workers. Similarly, the EU cases accept mandatory retirement as a means to avoid difficult end of career conversations that can result from loss of capacity, whilst the Canadian case law does not support such an approach.

Nonetheless, even in the case of the stricter protection against compulsory retirement found in the US and Canada, the cases suggest that the courts are fairly generous in their acceptance of age related justifications, and have accepted as justified treatment that can amount in practice to compulsory retirement. Thus, where staff are chosen for redundancy on the basis of cost, or proximity to pensionable age, this has been treated not as age discrimination *per se*, but as a separate reason, which is then found not to be unlawful.[296]

296 *Hazen Paper Co. v Biggins*, 507 U.S. 604 (1993).

The relative ease with which mandatory retirement practices can be justified in the EU and South Africa, including the acceptance in the EU of the concept intergenerational justice to explain the practice, reflects the fairly ready acceptance of the economic dimension to age equality. However, the economic and theoretical basis for this approach remains contested,[297] and so it is perhaps unsurprising that this is an area where the formal position differs significantly across different jurisdictions, with stricter approaches taken in North America.

Nonetheless, although explainable, the question of whether mandatory retirement is allowed would seem to be core to the understanding of age equality and the fact that there is no agreement on whether the practice should be banned clearly illustrates the lack of a coherent international response to problem of age discrimination.

The Dignity Paradox

All courts accept the need to address stigma and prejudicial stereotypes surrounding age, and they also accept that mandatory retirement can, with varying levels of ease, sometimes be justified. Another common theme is courts' uneasy approach to the role of dignity as an aim for equality law in age related cases. As referred to in Part 1, dignity is identified as a core aim for equality law, underpinning the rejection of prejudicial age based stereotypes. However, dignity can also justify some exceptions to age equality, either where treatment is based on the aim of avoiding undignified treatment as people age, or where less favourable treatment is allowed due to the absence of any attack on dignity.

This paradox is seen in the courts' varied treatment of age discrimination cases. For example, the CJEU and domestic courts in the EU have accepted as legitimate the aim of maintaining dignity for older workers by avoiding undignified performance management in later careers.[298] Such an approach relies on the stereotype that performance (and the insight to recognize this) deteriorates with age. A second example of the dignity paradox can be found in US and Canadian case law, where the absence of the infringement of dignity has been used to justify age discrimination. For example in the US case of *Hazen Paper Co. v Biggins*[299] the fact that the decision to dismiss was not based on inaccurate and stigmatizing stereotypes meant that it was easier to justify

297 See R. Horton, 'Justifying Age Discrimination in the EU' in U. Belavusau and K. Henrard, *EU Anti-Discrimination Law beyond Gender* (Hart Publishing, Oxford, 2018).

298 *Seldon v Clarkson Wright and Jakes* [2012] UKSC 16.

299 507 U.S. 604 (1993).

dismissing a worker; and in *Gosselin v. Québec*[300] the Canadian Charter of Rights and Freedoms was not breached when younger social assistance beneficiaries were treated less favourably, because younger people did not have any pre-existing disadvantage, stigmatisation or history of being undervalued.

The paradoxes inherent in relying on dignity arguments in relation to age, identified in Part 1, can therefore been seen in the case law of several jurisdictions, and can help explain some of the inconsistency in courts' approaches to age equality.

Recognising Structural Economic and Labour Market Dimensions

The review of the law in the different jurisdictions in chapter 2 provides many examples of the recognition by courts of the economic and structural dimensions to age equality. For example, those jurisdictions which protect young as well as older workers accept differential payments for younger workers on the basis that this can aid their entry into the workplace; and they also accept differential treatment in the case of compulsory redundancy and redundancy pay, to reflect the particular position of older workers with regard to their proximity to retirement. On the whole, then, the prohibition of age discrimination has had a limited disruptive effect on traditional labour market structures, and courts can be seen to accept established age based practices surrounding retirement and pay levels.

Whilst the different approaches of courts on the issues highlighted above can be understood to reflect the tension between economic and social aspects of age equality, they also can be seen to be a response to deeper aspects of labour market policy, beyond the immediate issue of age based practices.

For example, it is no surprise that South Africa with its acute concern for the position of younger workers, provides less protection for older workers than other states. Similarly, the difference in approach between the US and EU frameworks on age equality have been explained as reflecting different approaches to equality law more generally in the different jurisdictions. Thus, Suk suggests that in the US employment equality is closely tied to preserving individuals' choice to work, which explains why mandatory retirement ages are not accepted. In contrast, in Europe, employment equality 'requires collectively imposed norms about the role of work in a person's life,'[301] and so mandatory retirement schemes can be justified in the interests of younger workers.

---

300 [2002] 4 SCR 429.

301 J. Suk, 'From Antidiscrimination to Equality: Stereotypes and the Life Cycle in the United States and Europe' (2012) 60 (1) *The American Journal of Comparative Law* 75–98.

An alternative explanation of the different approaches, based on underlying labour market structures, is suggested by Kollonay Lehoczky, who points to the connection between the provision of discrimination protection and levels of legal protection for workers. Thus she points to the strong protection against mandatory retirement found in countries such as the US which provide weaker protection for older people beyond working age; and conversely that better social security provisions, such as those provided in many European countries, are often linked to a more permissive legislation and judicial approach to the retention of mandatory retirement.[302] The recognition that stronger age protection reflects weaker state provision is consistent with Somek's critique of equality law. He argues that equality law acts as a means to increase access to work by acting as a corrective to the barriers that otherwise exist to greater labour market participation by protected groups. The assumption behind this view is that subject to the protection of anti-discrimination law, the market can be left to operate with minimal state intervention.[303]

Although there may well be different base assumptions underpinning the social model and employment policies of different states, the difference in outcome in the different states should not be overemphasised however. The relatively relaxed standards of justification, based on reasonable business needs, means that in practice the US framework does not provide significantly dissimilar protection from other legal systems. For example, under the EU framework, retirement must be justified using labour policy reasons: in the US no special provision is made, but similar reasons could nonetheless be relied upon to justify the imposition of retirement in individual cases.

Ways Forward? A Multi-Dimensional Approach

The varied economic position as between different states, as well as their very different underpinning social policies, could be said to limit the value of the comparative exercise,[304] but nonetheless, the key social aspects of age equality, involving dignity and the removal of stigma and disadvantage, suggests that as with other human rights matters, comparative review remains of value.[305]

---

302 See C. Kollonay Lehoczky, Who, Whom, When, How? Questions and Emerging Answers on Age Discrimination, The Equal Rights Review (2013), Vol 11: 69–98.

303 See also the arguments proposed by A. Somek, Engineering Equality An Essay on European Anti-Discrimination Law (OUP, Oxford, 2011) discussed above at XXX.

304 O. Kahn-Freund, 'On Uses and Misuses of Comparative Law' (1974) 37 *MLR* 1.

305 On the extent to which judges use comparative legal perspectives in adjudicating human rights cases, see C. McCrudden, 'A Common Law of Human Rights? Transnational Judicial Conversations on Constitutional Rights' (2000) 20 *OJLS* 499.

What can be seen from this review is that despite different outcomes, the different jurisdictions hold in common their frequent efforts to reconcile the varied dimensions to age equality. To the variety of legal approaches reviewed in Part 2 can be added a further variation: the fact that many states have no legislative protection for age at all.

One interpretation of the variety in legal approaches is that it reflects the complexity and inconsistency inherent in the case for age equality discussed in Part 1; and the evidence from the review of different jurisdictions certainly provides numerous examples of internal inconsistency by the courts, such as the acceptance of 'collegiality' as a legitimate aim, despite its reliance on stereotypical assumptions about declining performance.

However, a more optimistic view of the current position is that, notwithstanding its limitations, the current legal frameworks contain the tools needed to address the shortcomings. This is because the notion of proportionality and reasonableness that are used extensively within the law on age equality can be used to take a multi-dimensional approach to equality, as advocated by Fredman,[306] in which the social and the economic aspects of age equality are seen in tandem.

Fredman suggests that the different dimensions of equality can interact, that the synergies and synthesis between them can help resolve difficult cases, and that recognition of the interaction of the different aims of equality can help better address the weaknesses of each claim. Her multi-dimensional approach is compatible with the current legal frameworks that are mostly based on notions of proportionality or reasonableness, and indeed, such a multi-dimensional approach can be seen to be emerging in the case law of different states. Fredman's approach provides a framework for assessing the weight of the different aspects of equality in any particular factual scenario,[307] and adds a more sophisticated and nuanced understanding of the range of factors that should feed into any assessment of proportionality or reasonableness.

In some contexts, the overriding concern may be to respond to the economic needs of demographic change, thereby justifying actions aimed at ensuring access to work for older or younger workers. Such an approach can explain the acceptance by the CJEU of the use of zero hours contracts only for those under

306 S. Fredman, 'Substantive Equality Revisited' (2016) 14(3) International Journal of Constitutional Law 712.

307 D. Schiek, 'Proportionality in Age Discrimination Cases: Towards a Model Suitable for Socially Embedded Rights' in A. Numhauser-Henning and M. Rönnmar (eds), *Age Discrimination and Labour Law: Comparative and Conceptual Perspectives in the EU and Beyond* (Kluwer, The Netherlands, 2015).

25 and over 55.[308] In other contexts, the purpose of age discrimination law may be to address dignitary and stigma harms, such as where individuals are subjected to other detriments due to age related stereotyping.[309] The acceptance by courts of a variety of aims and purposes for age discrimination law has the potential for creating nuanced and flexible legal responses.

One particular advantage to a multi-dimensional approach to addressing age equality is that it can be responsive to context, and can reflect the fact that the law does not operate in a vacuum. Thus courts may take into account in assessing whether an incident of age discrimination is justified, the background level of social protection provided in the society.[310] For example the existence of adequate state pension entitlements can be relevant to the assessment of justification.[311]

However, despite these strengths, a multi-dimensional approach also has the potential to create inconsistency, leading to the charge of incoherence. Even if the charge of incoherence can be dismissed, the plethora of factors that can be taken into account, let alone the fact that some such as dignity can be used on both sides in any balance, can mean that predictable outcomes are likely to be elusive. Moreover, the very fact that the different dimensions can all have valid and commendable aims, and yet pull in opposite directions, means that the decisions in the cases are always open to critique.

However, the proposal is not to create a formula to ensure that the resolution of age cases can be predicted in advance; nor to propose outcomes that are beyond critique. Instead Fredman's multi-dimensional approach can, as she suggests, create a set of evaluative criteria for determining the proper approach of courts in age equality cases. Whilst the current legal approaches considered above fall short of the nuanced approach advocated by Fredman, nonetheless the comparative review of the varied legal approaches to age equality does show the beginnings of a multi-dimensional analysis and elements of recognition of both social and economic limbs of equality. For example in *Seldon*[312] the UK Supreme Court recognises the structural and economic elements of equality, in its acceptance of the need for workforce planning, and intergenerational justice, but at the same time, it draws attention to the fact

308 See *Abercrombie & Fitch Italia Srl v. Antonino Bordonaro* Case C143/16, decision of AG Bobek on 23 March 2017.

309 *Kücükdeveci -v- Swedex GmbH & Co. KG* [2010] EUECJ C555/07.

310 C. Kollonay Lehoczky, Who, Whom, When, How? Questions and Emerging Answers on Age Discrimination, The Equal Rights Review (2013), Vol 11: 69–98.

311 *Felix Palacios de la Villa v Cortefiel Servicios SA* (Case C-411/05).

312 Seldon v Clarkson Wright and Jakes [2012] UKSC 16.

that reliance on collegiality as an aim may be contentious on the basis that it relies on prejudicial assumptions about capacity and age.

Equally, a multi-dimensional approach is not used as extensively as it might be: in particular, the review demonstrated an almost universal lack of acceptance of intersectional discrimination.[313] This is despite the fact that the protection of age equality would certainly be enhanced by a greater recognition by the courts of the concept of intersectionality with regard to age, in particular with the characteristics of gender and disability.

Despite its limitations in creating predictable and consistent outcomes in individual cases, a multi-dimensional approach may still be the best answer, albeit not perfect,[314] as to how to manage the range of factors that are in play in age equality cases. It involves an appreciation of the wide range of competing interests and the underpinning reasons for protecting age equality, and relies on reasoned and principled analysis to determine those factors which are relevant and how they should be balanced. Although there will always remain an area of discretion determining cases, it also requires that any decision be taken in full recognition of the competing interests at stake. In effect, such an approach requires a responsive approach on the part of courts to take account of the particular factual matrix in any particular situation.

Of course, while the social aims of equality, based on redressing disadvantage and stigma, are likely to remain stable, the economic and social context are likely to change over time. Thus demographic changes of increased longevity are likely to lead to structural changes, even if these are not mandated by the courts,[315] with the removal of state retirement ages already leading in some states to an extension in working lives.[316] In addition, the continued use of soft law to promote active ageing and to redress youth unemployment may lead to social change.[317] The economic situation can also change; economic recovery in states with high youth unemployment would shift the way in which disadvantage and intergenerational justice are used by courts in assessing whether

---

313 With the exception of South Africa.

314 See J.E. Fulcher, 'Using a Contextual Methodology to Accommodate Equality Protections along with the Other Objectives of Government (with Particular Reference to the Income Tax Act): "Not the Right Answer, Stupid. The Best Answer"' (1996) 34 *Alta LR* 416.

315 See M. Freedland and L. Vickers, 'Age Discrimination and EU labour rights law' in A. Bogg, C. Costello and A. Davies (eds), *A Research Handbook on EU Labour* Law (Cheltenham, Edward Elgar, 2016).

316 See page 6 for details of Canada's increased workforce aged 65–69.

317 For discussion of the active ageing agenda and actions of employers and social partners in addressing the active ageing agenda see S. Manfredi and L. Vickers, (eds.), *Challenges of Active Ageing: Equality Law and the Workplace*, Palgrave Macmillan UK (2016).

age discrimination is assessed. Changes to patterns of work, whether due to increased longevity, or increased mechanisation, are likely to affect working cultures and may also lead over time to a breaking down of age stereotypes as expectations and experiences of working life adjust. A legal approach which is capable of adapting and responding to culture and context is therefore essential.

This comparative review of legal responses to age equality provides evidence that there is still some way to go before sustainable and coherent legal responses to the issue of age equality can be achieved.[318] Yet the multi-dimensional approach to age equality advocated here is identifiable as present or at least emergent in the legal frameworks discussed, allowing space for these extra-legal changes in the social and economic context to be recognised in a responsive legal approach to age discrimination.

Bibliography

Alon-Shenker, P., 'The Duty to Accommodate Senior Workers: Its Nature, Scope and Limitations' (2012) 38 Queen's LJ 165.

Alon-Shenker, P., 'The Unequal Right to Age Equality: Towards a *Dignified Lives Approach* to Age Discrimination" (2012) XXV (2) *Canadian Journal of Law and Jurisprudence* 243.

Alon-Shenker, P., 'Legal Barriers to Age Discrimination in Hiring Complaints' (2016) 39 Dal LJ 289.

Anderson, S., 'What is the point of Equality?' (1999) 109(2) *Ethics* 287.

Barmes, L., Equality Law and Experimentation: The Positive Action Challenge (2009) 68 CLJ 623.

Barnard, C. and Hepple, B., 'Substantive Equality' (2000) 59 CLJ 562, S. Fredman, *Discrimination Law* (Oxford: OUP, 2002).

Belavusau, U. and Henrard, K., *EU Anti-Discrimination Law beyond Gender* (Hart Publishing, Oxford, 2018).

Bisom-Rapp, S. and Sargeant, M., 'Diverging Doctrine, Converging Outcomes: Evaluating Age Discrimination Law in the United Kingdom and the United States' (2013) 44 *Loyola University Chicago Law Journal* 717.

318 A. Numhauser-Henning and M. Rönnmar, 'Concluding Discussion' in A. Numhauser-Henning and M. Rönnmar (eds), *Age Discrimination and Labour Law: Comparative and Conceptual Perspectives in the EU and Beyond* (Kluwer, The Netherlands, 2015).

Bisom-Rapp, S. and Sargeant, M., 'It's Complicated: Age, Gender, and Lifetime Discrimination against Working Women—the United States and the U.K. as Examples' (2014) 22 Elder L.J. 1.

Blackham, A., 'Falling on Their Feet: Young Workers, Employment and Age Discrimination' (2015) 44(2).

Blackham, A., *Extending Working Life for Older Workers: Age Discrimination Law, Policy and Practice* (Hart Publishing, Oxford, 2016).

Bogg, A., Costello, C. and Davies A. (eds), *A Research Handbook on EU Labour* Law (Cheltenham, Edward Elgar, 2016).

Carlson, L., The Metamorphosis of Swedish Discrimination Law in Ahlberg, Källström, Malmberg, Koch (eds) *Vänbok till Ronnie Eklund* (Uppsala: Iustus, 2010).

Codagnone, C. and Martens, B., *Scoping the Sharing Economy: Origins, Definitions, Impact and Regulatory Issues* (European Commission, 2016).

Collins, H., 'Discrimination, Equality and Social Inclusion' (2003) 66 *MLR* 16.

Countouris, N., Freedland, M., (eds), *Resocialising Europe in a Time of Crisis* (Cambridge, CUP, 2013.

Crenshaw, K., 'Demarginalizing the Intersection of Race and Sex: A Black Feminist Critique of Antidiscrimination Doctrine, Feminist Theory, and Antiracist Politics', University of Chicago Legal Forum, 1989, 139.

Cupit, G., 'Justice, Age, and Veneration' (1998) 108 *Ethics* 702.

Dewhurst, E., 'Proportionality Assessments of Mandatory Retirement Measures: Uncovering Guidance for National Courts in Age Discrimination Cases' (2016) 45(1) *Industrial Law Journal* 60.

Doty, R., 'Age Discrimination in Employment Act and Mandatory Retirement of Law Firm Partners' (1979–80) 53 S. Cal. L. Rev. 1679.

Dupper, O. and Garbers, C. (eds), *Equality in the Workplace: Reflections from South Africa and Beyond (2009) Juta and Co. Ltd, Cape Town*).

Fraser, N., 'From Redistribution to Recognition? Dilemmas of Justice in a "Post-Socialist" Age' (1995) New Left Review 1/212 68.

Fraser, N., 'Rethinking Recognition' (2000) *3* New Left Review 107.

Fredman, S. and Spencer, S., *Age as an Equality Issue: Legal and Policy Perspectives* (Oxford: Hart Publishing, 2003).

Fredman, S., 'Substantive Equality Revisited' (2016) 14(3) International Journal of Constitutional Law 712.

Fredman, S., 'Women at Work: The Broken Promise of Flexicurity' (2004) 33 (4) *Industrial Law Journal* 299–319.

Fredman, S., *Intersectional Discrimination in EU Gender Equality and Non-Discrimination* (2016, European Commission, Brussels).

Fredman, S., The Future of Equality In Britain, EOC, Working Paper Series No. 5, (London, Equal Opportunities Commission 2002) 11.

Fulcher, H., 'Using a Contextual Methodology to Accommodate Equality Protections along with the Other Objectives of Government (with Particular Reference to the Income Tax Act): "Not the Right Answer, Stupid. The Best Answer"' (1996) 34 *Alta LR* 416.

Garbers, C., 'Discriminatory Dismissal' in Strydom (ed.) *Essential Employment Discrimination Law* (2012 Juta, Claremont).

Glenn, J.J. and Little K.E., 'A Study of the Age Discrimination in Employment Act of 1967' (2014) 31 GPSolo 41.

Grady, J., Trade Unions and the Pension Crisis: Defending Member Interests in a Neoliberal World, Employee Relations, (2013) Vol. 35 No. 3: 294–308.

Guralnik, J.M. and Leveille, S.G. et al., 'The impact of disability in older women' (1997) 52(3) J Am Med Womens Assoc. 113.

Harper, M.C., 'Reforming the Age Discrimination in Employment Act: Proposals and Prospects', (2012)16 Emp. Rts. & Emp. Pol'y J. 13.

Hellman, D. and Moreau, S., *Philosophical Foundations of Discrimination Law* (Oxford, OUP, 2013).

Hendrickx, F. (ed.), *Active Ageing and Labour Law* (2012, Intersentia, Cambridge).

Horan, M., 'The Supreme Court Retires Disparate Impact: Kentucky Retirement Systems v. EEOC Validates the Disparate Treatment Theory under the Age Discrimination in Employment Act' (2009) 29 J. Nat'l Ass'n Admin. L. Judiciary 115.

Jolls, C., 'Hands-tying and the Age Discrimination in Employment Act' (1996) 74 Tex. L. Rev. 1813.

Kahn-Freund, O., 'On Uses and Misuses of Comparative Law' (1974) 37 *MLR* 1.

Kant, E., *The Moral Law: Kant's Groundwork of the Metaphysics of Morals* (H J Paton, trans) (London, Hutchinson, 1963).

Karst, K., 'The Coming Crisis Of Work In Constitutional Perspective' [1997] Cornell LR 523, 532.

Khaitan, T., *A Theory of Discrimination Law* (Oxford, OUP, 2015).

Kilpatrick, C., 'The New UK Retirement Regime, Employment Law and Pensions' (2008) 37 ILJ 1.

Kollonay Lehoczky, C., Who, Whom, When, How? Questions and Emerging Answers on Age Discrimination, The Equal Rights Review (2013), Vol. 11: 69–98.

Lahey, JN., International Comparison of Age Discrimination Laws (2010) 32 (6) *Res Aging* 679.

Lazear, E.P., 'Why Is There Mandatory Retirement?' (1979) 87 *Journal of Political Economy* 1261–84.

Manfredi, S. and Vickers, L. (ed.), *Challenges of Active Ageing: Equality Law and the Workplace*, Palgrave Macmillan UK (2016).

Manfredi, S. and Vickers, L., 'Meeting the challenges of active ageing in the workplace: is the abolition of retirement the answer?' (2013) 4 (4) *European Labour Law Journal* 251.

Manfredi, S. and Vickers, L., 'Age equality and Retirement: squaring the circle' (2013) 42 (1) *Industrial Law Journal* 61.

McCrudden, C. (ed.), *Understanding Human Dignity* (Oxford, OUP, 2013).

McCrudden, C., 'A Common Law of Human Rights? Transnational Judicial Conversations on Constitutional Rights' (2000) 20 *OJLS* 499.

McKerlie, D., 'Equality and Time' (1989) 99 *Ethics* 475.

Neumark, D., 'The Age Discrimination in Employment Act and the Challenge of Population Aging,' (2009) 31 (1) *Research on Aging* 41–68.

Numhauser-Henning, A. and Rönnmar M. (eds), *Age Discrimination and Labour Law: Comparative and Conceptual Perspectives in the EU and Beyond* (Kluwer, The Netherlands, 2015).

Numhauser-Henning, A., An Introduction to Elder Law and the Norma Elder Law Research Environment, Different Approaches to Elder Law (2013) The Norma Research Programme Faculty of Law Lund University.

O'Cinneide, C., 'Fumbling Towards Coherence: The Slow Evolution of Equality and Anti-Discrimination Law in Britain' (2006) NILQ 57.

O'Cinneide, C. and Holder, J. (eds), *Current Legal Problems* (Oxford: OUP, 2008).

O'Connell, R., The role of dignity in equality law; lessons from Canada and South Africa (2008) 6(2) International J. Constitutional law 267.

Ortman, J.A., Velkoff, V.A., and Hogan, H., An Aging Nation: The Older Population in the United States Population Estimates and Projections Current Population Reports, Issued May 2014.

Pontz, E., 'What a difference ADEA makes: why disparate impact theory should not apply to Age Discrimination Act' (1995–6) 74 NCL Rev 267.

Prassl, J. and Risak, M., 'Uber, Taskrabbit, and Co.: Platforms as Employers-Rethinking the Legal Analysis of Crowdwork' (2015) 37 Comp. Lab. L. & Pol'y J.619.

Rawls, J., A Theory Of Justice (Oxford, OUP, 1999, revised edition).

Réaume, D., 'Discrimination and Dignity' (2003) 63 *Louisiana LR* 645, 675.

Reich, M., Gordon, D.M. and Edwards, R.C., 'Dual Labour Markets: A Theory of Labour Market Segmentation' (1982) 17 J Human Resources 359.

Rothenberg, J.Z. and Gardner, D.S., 'Protecting Older Workers: The Failure of the Age Discrimination in Employment Act of 1967' (2011) 38(1) *Journal of Sociology and Social Welfare* 9.

Rutherglen, G., 'From Race to Age: the Expanding Scope of Employment Discrimination Law (1995) 24(2) *The Journal of Legal Studies* 491.

Saldarriaga, S.M., 'Flaming Fifties and beyond: An International Comparison of Age Discrimination Laws and How the United States Could Improve the Laws for Elderly Women', (2017) 25 *Elder L.J.* 101.

Smith, B., *Intersectional Discrimination and Substantive Equality: A Comparative and Theoretical Perspective* (2016) 16 The Equal Rights Review 73.

Solanke, I., *Discrimination as Stigma: A Theory of Anti-Discrimination Law* (2017, Hart Publishing, Oxford).

Somek, A., *Engineering Equality An Essay on European Anti-Discrimination Law* (OUP, Oxford, 2011).

Suk, J., 'From Antidiscrimination to Equality: Stereotypes and the Life Cycle in the United States and Europe' (2012) 60 (1) *The American Journal of Comparative Law* 75–98.

Taylor, C., *Multiculturalism and The Politics of Recognition* (1992, Princeton University Press, Princeton).

Thornicroft, K., 'The Uncertain State of Mandatory Retirement in Canada' (2016) Labor Law Journal 397.

Westen, P., 'The Empty Idea of Equality' (1982) 95 Harv. L.R. 537.

Willetts, D., *The Pinch: How the Baby Boomers Took their Children's Future—And How they can Give it Back* (Atlantic Books, 2010).

Wirtz, W.W., The Older American Worker: Age Discrimination in Employment, Report of the Secretary of Labor to the Congress under Section 715 of the Civil Rights Act of 1964, (1965).

www.ingramcontent.com/pod-product-compliance
Lightning Source LLC
Chambersburg PA
CBHW031330230926
51848CB00001B/164

* 9 7 8 9 0 0 4 3 4 5 5 3 9 *